CW01652920

COMPLE ENGLISH

by

E. G. THORPE B.A.

BOOK THREE

Illustrated by

PRUE THEOBALDS

Heinemann

Heinemann Educational Publishers
Halley Court, Jordan Hill, Oxford OX2 8EJ
a division of Reed Educational & Professional Publishing Ltd

MELBOURNE AUCKLAND
FLORENCE PRAGUE MADRID ATHENS
SINGAPORE TOKYO SAO PAULO
CHICAGO PORTSMOUTH (NH) MEXICO
IBADAN GABORONE JOHANNESBURG
KAMPALA NAIROBI

ISBN 0 435 01887 6

First published 1963
96 97 98 26 25 24 23 22 21

By the same author

Complete English
INTRODUCTORY BOOK
BOOKS ONE TO FIVE

Separate Keys are available
for each book

Junior Dictionary
Illustrated Junior Dictionary

Produced by Mandarin Offset
Printed by Scotprint Ltd, Musselburgh, Scotland

Preface

This six-book English Course covers the following Junior School English: Comprehension, Language and Research (Spelling, Vocabulary, Dictionary work and Topics). It is intended for the consideration of teachers who believe that children come to school to work to the limit of their ability, that they should enjoy so doing through the provision of interesting work and that they should be encouraged to find out for themselves as far as possible by confident use of dictionary, atlas, reference books, etc.

Book III is for 3rd Year Junior quicker children and 4th Year slower children. There are thirty exercises, each divided into three parts; Comprehension, Language and Find Out.

Part I, *Comprehension*, has two sections: A (fairly easy) and B (more difficult), with 10 questions in each section.

The aim has been to present interesting, well-written passages of prose and poetry from a wide variety of authors and to set questions which require thought on the pupil's part, many questions requiring deduction from facts stated in the passage.

Children should be encouraged to think of their own title for each Comprehension passage.

Part II, *Language*, arises as far as possible from the Comprehension passage, each exercise having a main topic. The essential points of Grammar at this stage are covered, with constant revision throughout. Particular attention is given to common grammatical and spelling errors, increase of vocabulary and increased facility in the use of Language.

Part III, *Find Out*, encourages children to use dictionary, atlas, reference books, etc. There are four sections: (i) Words which cause confusion (similar spelling, etc.). (ii) Common expressions or colloquialisms. (iii) Homonyms. (iv) Research on a topic connected with the Comprehension passage.

The main topics dealt with in Parts II and III of each exercise are listed in summary form on the contents pages.

Acknowledgments

Thanks are due to the following authors, or their representatives and publishers, for permission to quote copyright material:

Brockhampton Press for *King of the Ice* from "Arctic Hunter" by Bud Helmericks;

Jonathan Cape Ltd. for *The Robbers' Prisoner* from "Redcap Runs Away" by Rhoda Power; *A Deafening Din* from "Volcano Adventure" by Willard Price.

Penguin Books Ltd. for *Sir Gawain and the Green Knight* from "King Arthur and His Knights of the Round Table" by Roger Lancelyn Green.

Oxford University Press for *Ships and Sharks* from "Son of Columbus" by Hans Baumann; *The King of the Blue Seas* from "Russian Tales and Legends" by Charles Downing; *A Secret Meeting* from "The Silver Branch" by Rosemary Sutcliff; *Fire!* from "Sama" by René Guillot; *The Harpist's Escape* from "Welsh Legends and Folk Tales" by Gwyn Jones.

George Harrap & Co. for *Avalanche!* from "Man of Everest" by J. R. Ullman.

Thomas Nelson & Sons Ltd. for *Binning's Trick* from "Scotland's Story" by H. E. Marshall; *Salmo* from "Round the Year Stories" by Maribel Edwin.

Macmillan & Co. Ltd. for *The Fishing Fleet's Return* from "Man from St. Malo" by R. D. Ferguson; *Flannan Isle* by Wilfred Gibson.

William Blackwood & Sons Ltd. for *The Highwayman* by Alfred Noyes.

The Bodley Head Ltd. for *Trying to Remember* from "Three Golden Nobles" by Christine Price.

Methuen & Co. Ltd. for *Old London Bridge* from "Ring out Bow Bells" by Cynthia Harnett.

Laurence Pollinger Ltd. and the estate of the late Mrs. Frieda Lawrence for *An Accident* from "The White Peacock" by D. H. Lawrence.

The extract from *Night Mail* by W. H. Auden is included by courtesy of H.M. Postmaster General.

Contents

1

King of the Ice

"We need plenty more seal," Oolak said as they parted. He added, "But you don't shoot seal in water now for they hard to get."

Two hours passed, during which Bob had heard Oolak's rifle crack four or five times. Bob decided to look for his companion and rejoin him. He climbed an ice pinnacle to look.

It was a peaceful scene that met Bob's gaze. White ice stretched before him with little streams flowing across its surface. The low hills and open plains of ice were all bathed in golden sunlight.

He did not see Oolak, but he became aware that the dogs had been howling for some time. It dawned on him that the entire team was in an uproar.

Glancing their way to see what the trouble was, his heart almost froze. Walking toward them was an immense whitish form, sleek head hanging low—a polar bear!

The bear smelled a freshly killed seal which Oolak had dragged to the sled, and it was this that he was seeking. To the clamour of the dogs he paid no more attention than if it were the buzzing of a fly. In his entire life the huge beast had never known fear, for the polar bear is the ruler of the ice. He knows no enemies.

From *Arctic Hunter* by Bud Helmericks

Comprehension

Always remember: **Use a Dictionary for Spelling and Meaning**

A 1. Why did Oolak take a gun when he went off alone?
2. Why did Bob climb an ice pinnacle?
3. Was it sunny, foggy, stormy or raining?
4. (a) What were the dogs doing? (b) Why?
5. What was lying by the sledge?
6. How did the bear know that there was food there?
7. What kind of team is mentioned: footballers, netball players, horses or sledge-dogs?
8. (a) Which two things were white? (b) What was golden?
9. (a) Had the seal been dead a long time? (b) How do you know?
10. What is the meaning of: companion, peaceful, flowing, immense, dragged, sled, seeking, enemies?

B 1. (a) What did Oolak say to Bob? (b) What did he mean?
2. What happened two hours after Oolak had left?
3. What was running across the ice: a bear, water, a dog, a fly?
4. (a) Who do you think Oolak was? (b) Why did he speak such strange English?
5. Who is called the King of the Ice?
6. Are polar bears fearless, cowardly, afraid of dogs, or friendly?
7. What annoyed the bear: a buzzing fly, the noisy dogs, the seal, or nothing?
8. What does this mean: "It dawned on him . . ."? Choose one of these answers: All this happened at dawn. Bob suddenly realised . . . The dawn came.
9. What does this mean: "To the clamour of the dogs he paid no more attention than if it were the buzzing of a fly."?
10. What is the meaning of: its surface, bathed in golden sunlight, in an uproar, his heart almost froze, sleek head, his entire life, an ice pinnacle?

Language

1. NOUNS

A word which tells us what we call something or someone is a NOUN.
Remember: A NOUN is a NAMING-WORD.

These are the names of things around you—desks, floor, ceiling, chairs, children, ruler, pen: all are NOUNS.

Write down six more nouns.

Ordinary names, like boy, girl, town, country, are called COMMON NOUNS.

Special names, beginning with a capital letter, like Roger, Sheila, London, England, are called PROPER NOUNS.

Remember: We can put *the*, *a* or *an* in front of Common nouns and it makes sense:

the boy   a girl   an apple

The noisy: this does not make sense because *noisy* is not a noun.

The noise: this makes sense. The word *noise* is a Common noun.

Pick out the Proper nouns: river, city, Manchester, John, River Clyde, hat, Australia, book, father, Mary, journey, North Sea, ocean.

2. Think of words which mean the same as these words: *little* streams, the *entire* team, uproar, glancing, immense, clamour, huge.
3. Think of words which mean the opposite of peaceful, white, little, low, huge, hills, froze, walking, immense, fresh, enemies, more.
4. Fill in the missing words, making the second pair agree in the same way that the first pair agree, like this: snow, white: coal, —— (Answer: black):

sun, sunshine,	:	moon, ——
snow, snowshoes	:	ice, ——
gold, golden	:	silver, ——
dog, puppy	:	bear, ——
team, sledgedogs	:	——, wolves
kind, cruel	:	——, enemies
polar bear, white	:	fox, ——
fly, buzzing	:	——, neighing

5. Choose the correct word:
   (a) Two hours (past, passed) before we heard anything.
   (b) We went (past, passed) the cinema just as the children were coming out.
6. (a) Think of two meanings of each word: ruler, plain, seal.
   (b) What is the difference in meaning between "Arctic Hunter" and an Arctic hunter?
7. (a) Put these in order of size: a spring, an ocean, the sea, a stream, a river.
   (b) What are these: a brook, a rivulet, a torrent, rapids?

8. *Find the Stranger:* Here is an example: eagle, crow, *fox*, swan (A *fox* is not a bird.)
Now do this one: polar bear seal sled dog

9. What do we call (a) very young dogs (b) baby bears (c) a dog's home (d) a bear's home (e) places where we can see bears in Britain?

10. Put into alphabetical order: gaze, bear, ice, fly, dog, hours, water, sun.

11. Write these sentences correctly:
We (was, were) going to the Zoo.
I shall (were, wear, where) my new overcoat.
You (was, were) out late last night.
(Where, Were, Wear, We're) are you going?

12. *Spelling* days: S . . . . . M . . . . . month: S . . . .
Look . nywhere you like, I don't mind.
I think the dogs have fo . . d s . . . thing in the hedge.

13. What do we call these marks: " " and when are they used?

14. Use the following in interesting sentences of your own:
an immense whitish form a peaceful scene in an uproar.

Find Out

1. Find out what these words mean, then use one from each group in sentences:
dragged, ragged, raged scene, scent, seen, sentence (2 meanings)
across, a cross, crossroads, crossbow aware, awake, award, awhile, await
streams, screams, streaks (2), strokes (2), streets, stretches, stretchers.

2. Find out the meaning of these sayings: like a bear with a sore head, bear up in time of trouble; show the white flag, white horses of the sea, as white as snow, as white as a sheet.

3. Think of words which sound the same (or nearly the same) but which are spelt differently, like *seas, sees* and *seize*: scene, plains, been, some, way, heart, bear.
Give the meaning of your words.

4. ARCTIC and ANTARCTIC
Use an atlas and a globe to find the Arctic Ocean and the Antarctic region. Which region is sea and which is land?
Find out about these explorers: Scott, Amundsen, Peary and Dr. Vivian Fuchs.

2

Choosing His Name

"He is exactly what John said, my dear. A pleasanter creature I never wish to mount. What shall we call him?"

"Would you like Ebony?" said she; "he is as black as ebony."

"No; not Ebony."

"Will you call him Blackbird, like your uncle's old horse?"

"No; he is far handsomer than old Blackbird ever was."

"Yes," she said, "he is really quite a beauty, and he has such a sweet, good-tempered face and such a fine, intelligent eye—what do you say to calling him Black Beauty?"

"Black Beauty—why, yes, I think that is a very good name. If you like, it shall be so;" and that is how I got my name.

When John went into the stable, he told James that master and mistress had chosen a good sensible English name for me that meant something; not like Marengo, or Pegasus, or Abdullah. They both laughed, and James said: "If it were not for bringing back the past, I should have named him Rob Roy, for I never saw two horses more alike."

"That's no wonder," said John. "Didn't you know that Farmer Grey's old Duchess was the mother of them both?"

I had never heard that before. So poor Rob Roy who was killed at the hunt was my brother!

From *Black Beauty* by Anna Sewell

Comprehension

A 1. What are the two people deciding?
2. They are talking about a (man, boy, blackbird, horse, book). Which?
3. (a) Are they looking at three horses and saying which one they like best?
(b) Why are Ebony and Blackbird mentioned?
4. Why do you think the uncle's old horse was called Blackbird?
5. Where did John go and what did he tell someone?
6. Were Marengo, Pegasus and Abdullah in the stable?
7. Who was the owner of Black Beauty's mother?
8. What was the name of Black Beauty's brother?
9. What had happened to him?
10. What do these words mean: a beauty, stable, master and mistress, alike?

B 1. (a) Who are talking at the beginning? (b) Who speaks first?
2. Why should they think of these special names: Ebony, Blackbird, Black Beauty?
3. Why did they not choose Blackbird as a name?
4. Why did they decide on the name Black Beauty?
5. How do we know that they thought this horse was fine-looking and clever?
6. Can you work out who John was and who James was?
7. How do we know that John was pleased with the name which had been chosen?
8. Why did he dislike the names Marengo, Pegasus and Abdullah?
9. Why did James think the horse might have been named Rob Roy?
10. What is the meaning of: to mount, ebony, intelligent, a good sensible English name, bringing back the past, That's no wonder, killed at the hunt?

Language

1. What is a noun? What is a Common noun? What is a Proper noun?
Think of five Common and five Proper nouns.
Put these nouns into two sets, Common or Proper nouns:
stable, girl, Susan, Robert, boy, John Smith, Liverpool, grey, Farmer Grey.

2. THE EXACT WORDS SPOKEN

Look at the conversation in the Comprehension passage *Choosing His Name.* THE EXACT WORDS SPOKEN go inside *Speech Marks:*

"Would you like Ebony?" she asked.

"No, not Ebony," he replied.

When someone opens the mouth to speak, we start the Speech Marks: ". . . .
When the person closes the mouth, we close the Speech Marks: . . . ."
Every word inside those Speech Marks was spoken: the exact words spoken.
Look at these two sentences:
(1) "I can't remember," he said. (2) He said that he could not remember.
The exact words spoken are in sentence 1. They are inside Speech Marks.
Sentence 2 does not tell us the exact words spoken, so NO Speech Marks are used.

Commas, full stops, question marks and exclamation marks always go *inside* the second Speech Marks:

"May I help you, please ?" I asked.

"Come here at once !" the policeman shouted.

Remember: (1) Speech Marks are called INVERTED COMMAS which means *upside-down* commas because the first ones are upside-down.
(2) When we write the exact words spoken, using inverted commas, we call it DIRECT SPEECH.

Write these sentences correctly:

(i) I don't like peculiar names for cats and dogs said my father
(ii) Why don't you hurry I asked my young brother
(iii) Lie down, you naughty dog I shouted

3. *Find the Stranger:* John David France Eric Stephen

4. Put into alphabetical order: exact, creature, mountain, each, everyone.

Remember: When words begin with the same letter, we must look at their second letter, like this: read, road: rE comes before rO, so *read* comes before *road.*

5. Make the second pair agree in the same way that the first pair agree:

crocus, flower	:	carrot, ——
man, woman	:	gentleman, ——
baby, babies	:	church, ——
knife, cutting	:	spade, ——
king, palace	:	lion, ——

6. What is the *male* (boy, man or father) of duchess, aunt, sister, queen, lady?

7. TEACH and LEARN

When the horse is being trained, he *learns*. His master *teaches* him. You go to school to *learn*. Your teachers *teach* you.

Use *teach* and *learn* in two sentences.

8. Write this correctly, putting, *to*, *two* or *too* in the spaces:

"If you are going —— the stables, may I come ——, as I would like —— see the —— horses, Ebony and Blackbird? I am —— scared —— go alone," said John.

9. Fill in the missing words (adjectives): England, English; Holland, ——; Germany, ——; Switzerland, ——; Australia, ——; Wales, ——; Scotland, ——; Ireland, ——; Denmark, ——; France, ——; Belgium, ——.

10. Use in sentences: past, passed, thrown, throne.

11. *Spelling* days: Tu . . . . . W . . . . months: Jan . . . . Feb . . . . .

There was a pic . . . . of a be . . tiful lady, over the fireplace.

Do you live in a bun . . . . . or a flat?

12. What are ALL the meanings of these words, like LIGHT which can mean *not dark* or *not heavy*: dear, mount, fine, saw?

13. What do these words mean: Singular and Plural? Give an example of each.

14. Use in interesting sentences: as black as ebony into the stable my brother.

Find Out

1. Find out what these words mean, then use one from each group in sentences:

exact, example, exaggerate, exclaim, explain sensible, senseless (2)

brother, bother, brother-in-law, broth, bronze, brooch pleasant, pheasant.

2. Find out the meaning of: horse-play, as strong as a horse, horse-flies, horse-chestnut, on horseback, horseshoes, horsemen, a sea-horse, horse-box.

3. Think of words which sound the same (or nearly the same) but which are spelt differently: dear, would, no, told, not, two, heard, so.

Give the meaning of your words.

4. HORSES

What are a stallion, mare, foal, colt, filly, mustang, racehorse, hunter, Shetland pony, stable, bridle, bit, saddle, reins, blinkers, stirrups?

3

The Squirrel

The pretty red Squirrel lives up in a tree,
A little blithe creature as ever can be;
He dwells in the boughs where the stock-dove broods,
Far in the shades of the green summer woods;
His food is the young juicy cones of the pine,
And the milky beech-nut is his bread and his wine.
In the joy of his nature he frisks with a bound
To the topmost twigs, and then down to the ground,
Then up again like a winged thing,
And from tree to tree with a vaulting spring;
Then he sits up aloft, and looks waggish and queer,
As if he would say, "Ay, follow me here!"
And then he grows pettish, and stamps his foot;
And then independently cracks his nut!
And thus he lives the long summer through,
Without a care or a thought of sorrow,
But, small as he is, he knows he may want
In the bleak winter weather, when food is scant:
So he finds a hole in an old tree's core,
And there makes his nest and lays up his store;
Then when cold winter comes and the trees are bare,
When the white snow is falling and keen is the air,
He heeds it not, as he sits by himself
In his warm little nest, with his nuts on his shelf.
O wise little squirrel! no wonder that he,
In the green summer woods, is as blithe as can be!

Mary Howitt

Comprehension

A 1. Where does the squirrel live?
2. (a) What else lives there? (b) What other name do we give to it?
3. What does the squirrel eat?
4. How can he seem to fly?
5. Is the squirrel lively, lazy, sad or sleepy in summer?
6. What does he do when he becomes bad-tempered?
7. Why does he find a hole in the tree?
8. What does he think of the winter cold and snow?
9. (a) What time of year is it at the start of the poem?
(b) When does he sit in his nest?
10. What do these words mean: dwells, boughs, frisks, topmost twigs, aloft, bleak winter weather, keen is the air?

B 1. The squirrel's tree is (in the middle of a field, in a hedgerow, deep in a wood, just outside a forest, just inside a wood). Which is right?
2. What is the wild bird doing? Do not use the poet's word.
3. How can beech-nuts be the squirrel's "bread and wine"?
4. What makes him run gaily up and down trees?
5. Can you think of an easier word than "scant" in line 18?
6. (a) To whom does the squirrel speak? (b) What does "Ay" mean?
7. If "independent" means you do not depend or rely on others, what do you think line 14 means?
8. "He knows he may want in the bleak winter weather . . ." Explain this.
9. Why is the squirrel happy in summer?
10. What is the meaning of: a little blithe (happy) creature as ever can be, in the joy of his nature, like a winged thing, a vaulting spring, waggish and quëer, then he grows pettish, an old tree's core, lays up his store, he heeds it not?

Language

1. Change to Direct Speech (the exact words spoken):
(i) The gay little squirrel told me to follow him up the tree.
(ii) I replied that I was very sorry but I could not climb so high.

2. SINGULAR and PLURAL

Singular means ONE: singular: *single.*

Plural means MORE THAN ONE: plural: *plus*: more.

Make a Singular list and a Plural list, putting these words into the proper list: squirrel, boughs, shades, woods, food, foot, he, trees.

Remember: Ways of forming plurals:

(1) add S: rat, rats rabbit, rabbits girl, girls.

(2) add ES to nouns ending in S, SH, CH or X: glass, glasses brush, brushes church, churches box, boxes

(3) change the ending F or FE to V and add ES: wolf, wolves knife, knives (Some words do not follow this rule: cliff, cliffs; chief, chiefs; etc.)

We shall remember other ways of forming plurals in the next exercise, Exercise 4.

Give the plural of squirrel, branch, switch, bush, fox, wife, cuff, calf.

3. Be sure that you understand the abbreviation ETC. which is used in Question 2 (Section called *Remember* 3). What does it mean and when do we use it?

4. What are the opposites of pretty, up, far, summer, young, juicy?

5. Find the words in the poem which rhyme with tree, pine, queer, store.

Which word here rhymes with *boughs*: bought, cows, coughs, trees, rough?

6. *Find the Stranger:* squirrel dove mole badger otter

7. Put *a* or *an* in front of these nouns: squirrel, dove, apple, orange, hour.

8. Make the second pair agree in the same way that the first pair agree:

people, houses	:	horses, ——
lion, roars	:	dog, ——
farmer, farm	:	teacher, ——
England, country	:	Cornwall, ——
laugh, happy	:	weep, ——
uncle, aunt	:	nephew, ——
oak, tree	:	apple, ——

9. *Spelling* months: J...... F....... A.... days: Th...... F.....

Will you ple... write the ad..ess clearly on the env.....?

Wear warm clo.... when clim.... high mount.... or you will be cold.

10. "And there makes his nest and *lays* up his store;"

Remember: Hens *lay* eggs. Mother *lays* the table.

I *lie* down now for a rest. I am *lying* down now.

I *lay* down a little while ago. I was *lying* down then.

Write these sentences correctly:

(i) "(Lay, Lie) down, you naughty puppy!" I shouted crossly.

(ii) Grandad was (laying, lying) down while we were (laying, lying) the tea-table.

(iii) I am going to (lay, lie) down while I am waiting.

11. Think of words which mean the same as these words: pretty, dwells, joy, *spring* up high, small, bleak, moist, courage.

12. Put into alphabetical order: squirrel, tree, nest, summer, winter, store.

13. Fill in the gaps with these times: at 9 a.m., at bedtime, on Saturday mornings, at dawn, between 12 o'clock and 1 p.m., remembering that a.m. means *before midday* and p.m. means *after midday*:

(i) I always feel wide awake —— but I have to go to bed.

(ii) I am always fast asleep ——.

(ii) We have our School dinner ——.

(iv) I play football ——.

(v) School Assembly begins ——.

14. Use in interesting sentences: bleak winter weather, the topmost twigs, green summer woods.

Find Out

1. Find out what these words mean, then use one from each group in sentences: summer, summit, simmer, slimmer, slimmest, slimy   bread, breadth   frisks, risks   through, threw, though   carefree, careful, careless.

2. Find out the meaning of: red-hot, caught red-handed, as red as a rose, as red as fire, a red herring, a red-letter day, like a red rag to a bull, to see red, the Red Cross; as green as grass, a greenstick fracture, a greenfinch, greengage, greengrocer, greenhouse, the greenwood, Greenland.

3. Think of words which sound the same (or nearly the same) but which are spelt differently: red, be, boughs, where, beech, bread, weather.

Give the meaning of your words.

4. WOODS

What are these: a sapling, plantation, clump, forest, copse, coppice, jungle, bush, an orchard, undergrowth, treetops, trunk, bough, branches, twigs?

4

On a Mountain-side

The valley lay far below, bathed in the sparkling morning sunshine. In front of Heidi a big, broad snowfield rose up to the dark blue sky and on the left stood a huge pile of rocks above which a bare rocky peak reached towards the sky, towering majestically above the child.

Heidi sat motionless. A great silence was all around and only the delicate blue harebells and yellow cistus swayed softly in the gentle breeze, nodding joyfully on their slender little stems. Peter had fallen asleep and the goats were climbing high up among the bushes. Heidi had never been so happy. The golden sunlight, the fresh breezes and the delicate perfume of the flowers filled her with delight and she only wished that she might stay there for ever. She gazed so long at the mountains that it seemed to her that each had a face and that these mountain-faces were as familiar to her as old friends.

Suddenly Heidi heard a loud, harsh cry and when she looked up she saw, circling overhead, a huge bird, larger than she had ever seen before. His large wings were outspread and he flew in a wide circle, coming back again and again and uttering loud, piercing shrieks above Heidi's head.

From *Heidi* by Johanna Spyri

Comprehension

A 1. Where was Heidi?
2. What was lit up by the sunshine?
3. What time of day was it?
4. Who was with Heidi?
5. What faces did Heidi look at: the faces of climbers, goats' faces, imaginary faces or schoolfriends' faces?
6. What noise did she suddenly hear?
7. How do we know that Heidi was young?
8. Where did she wish to stay for ever?
9. What did she stare at for a long time?
10. What is the meaning of: huge, silence, harebells, cistus, breeze, slender?

B 1. What do you think was Peter's job?
2. Which three things pleased Heidi?
3. What bird do you think it was overhead?
4. If the correct way to speak to a king or queen is to say "Your Majesty" and "towering" means "standing like a tall tower", what do you think this means: "towering majestically above the child."?
5. (a) What does this mean: ". . . these mountain-faces were as familiar to her as old friends."?
   (b) How could she imagine faces there?
6. What was (a) dark blue (b) light blue (c) yellow (d) white (e) golden?
7. Who (a) did not move (b) slept?
8. What (a) climbed (b) shrieked?
9. Can you guess why the bird was flying overhead and shrieking?
10. What is the meaning of: bare rocky peak, motionless, delicate perfume, flew in a wide circle, piercing shrieks, fresh breezes, sparkling, nodding joyfully?

Language

1. Give the plural of snowfield, thief, handkerchief, shelf, church, wolf, match.
2. SINGULAR and PLURAL 2

In Exercise 3 we remembered three ways of forming plurals: (1) add S, (2) add ES, (3) change F or FE to V and add ES. Other ways are:

(4) add S to words ending with a vowel and Y: day, days key, keys
no vowel before Y, change Y to I and add ES: baby, babies lady, ladies

(5) change the vowels in the middle: tooth, teeth man, men

(6) add a new ending: child, children ox, oxen

(7) no change at all: sheep, sheep deer, deer

Be careful with words ending in O: piano, pianos solo, solos echo, echoes potato, potatoes tomato, tomatoes

What is the plural of army, fly, monkey, city, chimney, boy, child, sheep, halo?

3. Which letters of the alphabet are vowels?
Letters which are not vowels are called CONSONANTS. How many are there?

4. Change these words into nouns, like this: brave, *bravery*:
sparkling, broad, dark, joyfully, loud, harsh, circling, happy.

You can check your nouns by putting *the* in front and seeing if it makes sense: *The* bravery of the man . . .

5. *Find the Stranger:* soft silent motionless asleep piercing

6. Make sense out of these jumbled words:
(i) the Heidi was mountain very happy on.
(ii) sat the in still She sunlight quite golden.
(iii) were away asleep and Peter goats wandering was his.

7. Write correctly:
(i) (As, Has) soon (has, as) she (as, has) found her coat, we shall go.
(ii) (As, Has) your father received my letter?
(iii) The cunning fox (is, his) trying to find (is, his) dinner.
(iv) (Is, His) this (is, his) lost cap?

8. Make the second pair agree in the same way that the first pair agree:

shoes, laces	:	coat, ——
mountain, summit	:	waves, ——
silence, noise	:	silent, ——
tears, sadness	:	laughter, ——
red, squirrel	:	——, mole
afternoon, evening	:	night, ——
grandfather, grandmother	:	man, ——
uncle, aunt	:	——, niece

9. "The valley lay far below, bathed in the *sparkling* morning sunshine."
   Use three of these *brightness* words in interesting sentences:
   blazing, glossy, brilliant, dazzling, gleaming, shining, twinkling.
10. *Spelling* months: O...... N....... D....... day: S.......
   There are many co..ties in our c...try, the largest being Y...shire.
   It was very quiet and p....ful, walking with my fr..nd in the f..lds.
11. Put into alphabetical order: big, broad, beside, bathed, breezes.
   If some words begin with the same two letters, like catch, cabbage, we have to look at their third letters: ca*B* comes before ca*T*, so *cabbage* is before *catch*.
12. Heidi is a girl (female), Peter is a boy (male). What do we call the male and female of these: cattle, geese, rabbits, foxes, people, pigs, fowls?
13. What does this word mean: Punctuation?
   Write a sentence in which someone asks a question. Underline all punctuation marks in your sentence.
14. Use in interesting sentences: sparkling morning sunshine rocky peak a loud, harsh cry.

Find Out

1. Find out what these words mean, then use one from each group in sentences:
   delicate, deliberate, delicious
   sparkled, speckled, spotted (2)
   field, fieldfare, fiend, fierce, fiery
   blue, blew, blow (2)
   valley, volley, volume (2), value, valueless, valuable, invaluable.
2. Find out the meaning of: a sunbeam, sun-blind, sunburn, sunshade, sun-dial, sunset, sunrise, sunflower, sunstroke, sunny, a month of Sundays; a golden wedding, as good as gold, a golden opportunity, a goldfish, goldfinch, goldsmith, Golden Eagle, Silence is golden. All that glitters is not gold.
3. Think of words which sound the same (or nearly the same) but which are spelt differently: flower, which, bare, their, morning, seemed, saw, flew.
   Give the meaning of your words.
4. SWITZERLAND
   Find Switzerland in your atlas and on the globe. Which countries are next to it? What are the Alps, St. Bernard dogs, chalets, avalanches, cow-bells? What do the Swiss make, which we can then buy in our country? Who was William Tell?

A Mischievous Boy

One day his aunt's yellow cat came along, purring, eyeing the teaspoon and begging for a taste. Tom said:

"Don't ask for it unless you want it, Peter."

But Peter signified that he did want it.

"You better make sure."

Peter was sure.

"Now you've asked for it, and I'll give it to you, because there ain't anything mean about *me*; but if you find you don't like it you mustn't blame anybody but your own self."

Peter was agreeable, so Tom pried his mouth open and poured down the Pain-killer. Peter sprang a couple of yards into the air, and then delivered a war-whoop and set off round and round the room, banging against furniture, upsetting flower-pots, and making general havoc. Next he rose on his hind feet and pranced around, in a frenzy of enjoyment, with his head over his shoulder and his voice proclaiming his happiness. Then he went tearing around the house again, spreading chaos and destruction in his path. Aunt Polly entered in time to see him throw a few double summersets, deliver a final mighty hurrah, and sail through the open window, carrying the rest of the flower-pots with him. The old lady stood petrified with astonishment, peering over her glasses; Tom lay on the floor, expiring with laughter.

"Tom, what on earth ails that cat?"

"*I* don't know, Aunt," gasped the boy.

"Why, I never seen anything like it. What *did* make him act so?"

" 'Deed I don't know, Aunt Polly; cats always act so when they're having a good time."

From *The Adventures of Tom Sawyer* by Mark Twain

Comprehension

A 1. Peter was (Tom's best friend, Tom's uncle, a cat, Aunt Polly's dog). Which?
2. Why did Peter race round the room?
3. Who was Peter's owner?
4. Which way did Peter go out of the room?
5. (a) What did he knock over as he went out? (b) Had he knocked any over before?
6. Who was very amused by the cat's behaviour?
7. Who asked what was the matter with the cat?
8. Who said that the cat was enjoying itself?
9. What was Tom's surname?
10. What is the meaning of: purring, eyeing, anything mean, a war-whoop, furniture, enjoyment, tearing around?

B 1. What is the meaning of: "his voice proclaiming his happiness"?
2. What is our proper name for "Pain-Killer"?
3. Why did the cat beg?
4. How did Peter do this: ". . . signified that he did want it."?
You can guess the meaning of "signified" from the beginning of the word.
5. Havoc, chaos and destruction all mean the same thing in this story. What?
6. Why do you think the old lady peered *over* instead of *through* her glasses?
7. Why was Tom lying on the floor when she came in?
8. (a) Who asked two questions? (b) What did the person wish to know?
9. (a) Do you believe the storyteller when he writes "a frenzy (madness) of *enjoyment* . . . his *happiness* . . ."? (b) Say why the cat behaved so strangely.
10. What is the meaning of: eyeing the teaspoon, Peter was agreeable, pried his mouth open, hind feet, double summersets (double somer . . . . . s), petrified ("turned to stone") with astonishment, expiring ("dying") with laughter, ails (a doctor is interested in our "ailments")?

Language

1. What is the plural of baby, valley, woman, deer, child, sheep, piano, cargo?
2. PUNCTUATION

Putting the various stops like full stops and commas into writing is called PUNCTUATION.

Say what we call each of these "stops": ! ? " " . ,

Remember: These stops or marks are called PUNCTUATION MARKS.

Write this, filling in the gaps: We start sentences with ——— and at the end we put ———. When we pause for breath in a sentence we put ———.

Remember: (1) Do NOT put a comma before the word *and*: jam, honey and cake

(2) Titles of books and poems go inside inverted commas, with capital letters except for short words: "The Adventures of Tom Sawyer" but printers put titles in *italics*: *Heidi* by Johanna Spyri.

(3) Anything copied from a book or poem goes inside inverted commas (then called QUOTATION MARKS) to show that it has been copied and that we have not thought of it ourselves.

(4) In Direct Speech (the exact words spoken) punctuation marks like commas, full stops, question and exclamation marks go *inside* the second inverted commas:

"What do you want?" he asked.

Write correctly, putting in capital letters and punctuation marks:

(a) have you seen the cat asked aunt polly

(b) lie down peter tom shouted

(c) the squirrel is the title of a poem by mary howitt

3. *Find the Stranger:* Tom John Dennis Aunt Roger

4. Pick out of the brackets a word which belongs to the word on the left, like this: snow (slow, *flakes*, black, knows) *flakes* belong to snow.

ladder	(bells, rungs, lad, lady)
bed	(red, roof, blankets, window)
trees	(freeze, branches, three, daffodils)
kitchen	(sleeping, cooking, shopping, kitten)
feet	(hands, toes, nose, fingers)

5. In the book about Tom Sawyer, Tom and Aunt Polly make mistakes when they speak. Correct these:

(a) "You better make sure." (b) ". . . there ain't anything mean about me."

(c) "Why, I never seen anything like it."

6. *Spelling* months: N . . . . D . . . . workers: po . . man pol . . . man

The doctor examined my ton . . . and thr . . . carefully.

I tho . . . t you would not come thr . . . . that dark wood. Were you afr . . .?

7. Put into alphabetical order: cat, furniture, sure, floor, chaos.
8. Think of words which mean the same as these words: pried open, sprang, a couple of, upsetting something, *hind* legs, enjoyment, entered, final.
9. Give the opposites of came, sure, give, anything, find, like, happiness, entered, open, laughter.
10. Write correctly:
    (i) (Has, As) Tom's aunt did not (no, know, now) what was wrong with the cat, she (asked, told) Tom what was (the, a) matter.
    (ii) Tom (asked, told) his aunt that all cats jumped about for (joy, sorrow).
11. What are these "houses": a greenhouse, lighthouse, summer-house, hot-house, bakehouse, warehouse?
12. What are *all* the meanings of hind, mean, rose, tearing, general and pried?
13. What are adjectives? Find three in the passage about Tom Sawyer.
14. Use in interesting sentences: havoc the open window peering over her glasses.

Find Out

1. Find out what these words mean, then use one from each group in sentences:
    tea (2), teaspoon, teaspoonful   shoulder, should, soldier, solder
    purring, spurring, stirring (2), staring, starry, tarry (2)   peering, peeping
    window, widow, widower   thrown, throne   single, double, treble.
2. Find out the meaning of: a yellow-hammer; to let the cat out of the bag, a cat burglar (why?), a cat and dog life, raining cats and dogs, like a cat on hot bricks, a cat's eyes, cats'-eyes (Road Safety), a cat-o'-nine-tails, a cat-nap, When the cat's away, the mice will play.
3. Think of words which sound the same (or nearly the same) but which are spelt differently: I'll, there, pried, feet, see, know, boy.
    Give the meaning of your words.
4. WILD CATS
    What do we call the female and young of lions, leopards and tigers?
    What are these "wild cats": a jag . . ., pu . ., cou . . ., pan . . . ., che . . . . and ly . . and in which countries do they live?

6

Sir Gawain and the Green Knight

The drawbridge was let down, the gate flung wide, and Gawain rode out of the castle, with a squire to guide him. Through the bitter dawning they rode, beneath trees dripping drearily, and across meadows where the wind moaned as it bit them to the bone, and they came to a great valley with cliffs at one side of it, all filled with mist.

"Sir," said the squire, "go no further, I beg of you. Near here dwells the Green Knight, a terrible and a cruel man. There is none so fierce or so strong in this land—and no man may stand against him. Over yonder at the Green Chapel it is ever his custom to stay all who pass by, and fight with them, and kill them—for none can escape him. Flee away now—and I will not tell ever that you fled for fear of the terrible Green Knight."

"I thank you," said Gawain, "but I must go forward. I would be a coward and unworthy of knighthood if I fled away now. Therefore, whether I like it or not I must go forward . . . And God knows well how to save His servants if so He wills."

"Well then," said the squire, "your death be your own doing. Go down this path by the cliff, into the deep valley, and upon the left hand, beyond the water, you will find the Green Chapel. Now farewell, noble Gawain, for I dare not come with you further."

Down the path rode Gawain, and came to the bottom of the valley. No chapel could he see, but only the rugged cliff above him, and high, desolate banks in the distance. But at length he saw, under the dripping trees, a low green mound beside the rushing stream; and he heard a sound as of a scythe upon a grindstone coming from a deep hollow in that mound.

From *King Arthur and his Knights of the Round Table*

by Roger Lancelyn Green

Comprehension

A 1. Who showed Gawain the way?
2. (a) What was lowered? (b) What was opened?
3. What time of day was it: evening, dawn, midnight, midday or afternoon?
4. What was the weather like?
5. What danger lay ahead?
6. Where was the path down into the valley?
7. What would Gawain have to cross to find the Green Knight?
8. Who went with Gawain down into the valley?
9. How did Gawain go down into the valley: on foot, on horseback, crawling or running?
10. What is the meaning of: knight, terrible, cruel, over yonder, noble Gawain, coward, dwells?

B 1. (a) Who begged someone not to proceed? (b) Why?
2. Where were they at that moment?
3. (a) Where did the Green Knight stop all travellers? (b) Why did he stop them?
4. How can you tell that Gawain was a stranger and did not live nearby?
5. Say what (a) were wet, (b) were windswept, (c) was biting, (d) was misty.
6. (a) Was the valley a gloomy or a cheerful place? (b) How do you know?
7. (a) Did Gawain hear a scythe being sharpened? (b) How do you know?
8. Who do you think was in the deep hollow and what was he doing?
9. (a) What was the Green Chapel, really? (b) Why do you think it was so called?
10. What is the meaning of: drawbridge, squire, the bitter dawning, trees dripping drearily, rugged cliff, desolate banks, scythe, grindstone?

Language

1. Write these sentences correctly:
   (i) sir gawain one of king arthurs knights was very brave
   (ii) the adventures of tom sawyer was written by mark twain
   (iii) I have just read a book entitled ——— by ———. (Fill the spaces.)

2. ADJECTIVES

An *adjective* is a *describing word:* beautiful, ugly, brave.

Adjectives tell us more about nouns: a *beautiful* dress, the *Ugly* Sisters in the pantomime, the *brave* soldier, *stormy* winds, a *rough* sea.

Here are six adjectives: bitter, terrible, green, deep, ragged, kind.

Give a noun to each one, like this: ragged children.

Remember: (1) Adjectives DESCRIBE, making a story more vivid and interesting.

(2) Use descriptive adjectives, not dull ones like *nice, good, great* or *funny*: a nice day, nice present, nice drink, nice or good book, a good long walk, good baby, good film, good programme, a great game, great shout, a great big bang, a funny book, a funny thing happened, funny face, etc.

The adjectives *nice, good, great* and *funny* do not describe the things at all.

Think of more interesting adjectives to describe all the nouns in the list which you have just read, like this: a sunny day, useful present, refreshing drink.

(3) Always find *many* different adjectives which describe the same sort of thing, so that you do not have to keep using the same adjective. Instead of *angry*, you can use annoyed, cross, enraged, furious, fuming, indignant, infuriated, irate, raging, wrathful, etc.

Make up a similar list for *afraid.*

3. *Find the Stranger:* trees meadows cliffs knight banks

4. Put into alphabetical order: desolate, distance, dripping, down, death, deep.

5. Use in sentences: mist, missed.

6. Give the plural of chapel, church, valley, army, thief, hero.

7. What are these jobs: judge, mechanic, optician, joiner, cobbler?

8. *Spelling* workers: plu . . er por . . . young ones: fa . . (deer) f . . l (horse)
Jackdaws are often misch . . . ous and n . . . . ty birds.
How I lost my raincoat is qui . . a m . stery to me.

9. SILENT K: What are these words which have a silent K, like KNIGHT:
(i) used for cutting (ii) to tap or hit (iii) part of the leg (iv) to be sure of something (v) done with long needles (vi) often part of a door (vii) you can tie one (viii) part of the hand?

10. Write these sentences correctly:

(1) The two (enemy's, enemies) met face to face.
(2) Mother (nose, knows) that we are in a (great, grate) hurry.
(3) All the children (new, knew) the (write, right) answer.
(4) I like (them, those, that) apples best of all.

11. ALL ARE WHAT? What are they all on each line (animals or birds, etc.)?

cub, kitten, gosling, lamb, chick
? . , ! " " '
tinkle, crash, gurgle, splash, clap
cello, violin, piano, trumpet, drum
crimson, green, white, black, blue
jungle, wood, forest, clump, copse
scythe, sickle, knife, shears, scissors
uncle, aunt, nephew, niece, cousin

12. What is the difference between these buildings: a house, bungalow, flat, shack, palace, cottage, hovel, hut?

13. What is a verb? Write a sentence and underline the verb.

14. Use in interesting sentences: out of the castle filled with mist high, desolate banks.

Find Out

1. Find out what these words mean, then use one from each group in sentences:
custom, customer, custard squire (2), Esquire (Esq.), squirm, squirt, squelch
coward, cowherd, cowardly, cowardice terrible, terrified horrible, horrified.

2. Find out the meaning of: high days and holidays, left high and dry, in high glee, to ride the high horse, search high and low, high-pitched, the high seas, high spirits, high tide, high summer, high tea, high treason, It's high time we went home.

3. Think of words which sound the same (or nearly the same) but which are spelt differently: or, knight, but, whether, rode, side, find, here, flee.
Give the meaning of your words.

4. KING ARTHUR'S KNIGHTS
Find out all you can about the legends of King Arthur. Was there a real King Arthur? Who or what were the Round Table, Sir Lancelot, Merlin, Guinivere, Excalibur, Tintagel Castle and Avalon?

7

Escape at Bedtime

The lights from the parlour and kitchen shone out
    Through the blinds and the windows and bars;
And high overhead all moving about,
    There were thousands and millions of stars.
There ne'er were such thousands of leaves on a tree,
    Nor of people in church or the Park,
As the crowd of the stars that looked down upon me,
    And that glittered and winked in the dark.

The Dog, and the Plough, and the Hunter, and all,
    And the star of the sailor, and Mars,
These shone in the sky, and the pail by the wall
    Would be half full of water and stars.
They saw me at last, and they chased me with cries,
    And they soon had me packed into bed;
But the glory kept shining and bright in my eyes,
    And the stars going round in my head.

Robert Louis Stevenson

Comprehension

A 1. At what time of day did this happen: morning, afternoon, night or dawn?
2. If you stood outside the house in this poem, what would you see?
3. Where were the lights?
4. What sparkled in the darkness?
5. What does the word "cries" mean in the second verse?
6. What are (a) the Dog (b) the Plough (c) the Hunter?
7. How could stars lie in a pail of water?
8. How can stars go round in your head?
9. How do we know that there was a great multitude of stars?
10. What is the meaning of: parlour, kitchen, blinds, glittered, winked, pail?

B 1. "Escape at Bedtime": escape from what?
2. How old do you think the person is who is telling this story? (Not the poet) Why do you think so?
3. Why does this person talk about leaves and people?
4. How can we tell that this person is *very* interested in stars?
5. (a) Which is the "star of the sailor"? (b) Why?
6. "They saw me at last, and they chased me with cries . . ."
(a) Who did? (b) Why? (c) What do you think they shouted?
7. What was the glory?
8. How could the glory keep "shining" and be "bright in my eyes"? Choose an answer: I was staring at the stars. I crept out of bed to look again. I had been staring so long at the stars that they seemed to be spinning round in my head. My eyes shone brightly.
9. What was the sky like? Choose two adjectives: cloudy, clear, sunny, starry.
10. What is the meaning of: through the blinds, Mars, ne'er, packed into bed, the crowd, going round in my head?

Language

1. Think of a suitable adjective for each of these three nouns, then use your answers in sentences: kitchen, stars, crowd.
Here is an example: crowd: A *noisy* crowd was waiting outside the prison.

2. VERBS

A VERB is a DOING-WORD or ACTION: I *run*, I *am running*, was running, ran, have run, had run, shall run.

These actions take place at different *times*: (1) *now: present* (2) *then: past* (3) *still to come: future*.

Pick out the verbs and say whether they are in the Present, Past or Future time:

(i) The stars looked down on me and glittered and winked.

(ii) I shall send an answer tomorrow.

(iii) We give you this reward with very great pleasure.

(iv) John has caught a cold.

Remember: The proper name for verb *times* is TENSES: Present tense, Past tense, Future tense.

3. What do we call the places where these are made: beer, flour, ships, bread? What do we call the shops where these are sold: bread, milk, vegetables, meat?

4. Give one word for each group of people: (a) in church or chapel (b) in a theatre or concert hall (c) at a football match (d) waiting in line for a bus.

5. (a) Which words in the poem rhyme with out, dark, Mars, eyes?
(b) Which of these words rhymes with *fought*: through, fight, caught, right?

6. *Find the Stranger:* parlour kitchen garage bedroom bathroom

7. *Spelling* I looked stra. . . t ahead, over the roo. . of the houses in our str. . t, past the factory chim. . . s, to the starry sky. I saw the Plough, glit. . . ing and spar. . ing merr . . ., with the North Star nearby, the fr . . nd and helper of sai . . . . at sea.

8. Choose the right words:

(i) Why did the girls leave (their, there) needlework over (their, there)?

(ii) (Here, Hear, Ear) is your homework.

(iii) Can you (here, hear, ear) a faint, scratching noise?

(iv) "(There, Their, They're) coming up the hill now!" I shouted excitedly.

9. Write in the plural, changing all singular words:

(i) Our church is very old.

(ii) The beech does not grow on the beach.

(iii) Give the knife to the boy who is most careful.

(iv) A grand piano is expensive.

(v) There is a very clear echo in the cave in the valley.

10. Make pairs of words with the same meaning, like *hit*, *strike*: *hit*, foliage, end, pursue, magnificent, sparkle, finish, leaves, glitter, naughty, chase, mischievous, splendid, *strike*.

11. Think of words for the amount which *fills* a spoon, a bucket, a cup, a glass and a basket, taking care how you spell the words: a spoon . . ., etc.

12. The three on the left ALL HAVE *one* of the things in the brackets. Which one?

human beings, animals, birds	:	(wings, tails, legs, beaks)
parlour, kitchen, bedroom	:	(walls, fires, beds, settees)
church, chapel, cathedral	:	(archbishops, clock-towers, congregations)
dog, elephant, tiger	:	(owners, limbs, kennels, collars)
stream, river, sea	:	(ships, bridges, water, tunnels)
eyes, schools, teachers	:	(eyelashes, pupils, rooms, children)

13. What is an adverb? Write down three, then use one of them in a sentence.

14. Use in interesting sentences: through the window   high overhead   thousands of leaves.

Find Out

1. Find out what these words mean, then use one from each group in sentences:
   crowd, crowed, crowned, crown (2)   sky, ski   stars (2), stares, stairs
   glitter, litter (2), listen, glisten   light (2), alight, height, tight
   plough, rough, cough, though, through, thorough (note the different sounds).

2. Find out the meaning of: kept in the dark, keep something dark, look on the dark or black side; bring someone round (2), come round (2), to round off, to round on someone, a round trip, to round up.

3. Think of words which sound the same (or nearly the same) but which are spelt differently: were, nor, in, pail.

   Give the meaning of your words.

4. STARS

   Find out the names of well-known groups of stars or single stars, like the North Star, the Plough and the Hunter.

   How can we find the North Star? Why was this star very important to sailors in olden days?

8 *The Robbers' Prisoner*

Inside the sack, Redcap was breathing heavily. His face and neck were wet with heat and the swinging of his body, hanging by his belt from the pole, made him feel sick. He had no idea of where he was being taken and he could not guess how much time had passed since the robbers had seized him. In his distress, he had forgotten about Nial and the other minstrels and about Red Eric, whom he had set out to find. He thought only of his own village, the friendly glow of the fire in his father's forge, and his own safe bed of straw in the corner of the cottage, where he and his parents had always slept so near to each other.

"I shall never see home again," he thought, "never, never. What shall I do?" He was almost crying, but he kept back his tears and tried in vain to think of some way of escape.

Suddenly, his misery was interrupted by a bump and he felt himself lying on his back on the ground while somebody pulled the pole out of his belt and clumsy hands dragged the sack from his head.

An ugly unshaven face, with a pair of very small brown eyes and a black gap where the front teeth should have been, was bending over him. Two hairy hands under his armpits placed him upright in a sitting posture and a voice growled, "Sit quiet and you may be given something to eat. Try to stand or shout and you'll go back hungry into the sack."

From *Redcap Runs Away* by Rhoda Power

Redcap Runs Away is a story about life in England around 1350.

Comprehension

A 1. Where was Redcap?
2. Why did he feel sick?
3. Where was the sack?
4. What had Redcap forgotten?
5. (a) Whom did he want to find? (b) Can you guess why?
6. Did Redcap suddenly see his father?
7. (a) What did he fear he would never see again? (b) Why?
8. What did a sudden bump interrupt?
9. Describe the man who told Redcap to keep quiet.
10. What is the meaning of: wet with heat, his belt, the pole, robbers, seized, way of escape, friendly glow, his own safe bed of straw?

B 1. How could Redcap be in a sack and hanging at the same time by his belt from a pole?
2. Why was Redcap breathless and uncomfortable?
3. Did he know (a) where he was going (b) how long he had been a prisoner (c) where Red Eric was (d) how to escape (e) that he was in the hands of thieves?
4. Why had he forgotten about the minstrels?
5. Why do you think he suddenly thought about his home?
6. What did his father do for a living?
7. Which words tell us that Redcap could not think of a way of escape?
8. Why do you think the man Eric was called Red Eric?
9. How was Redcap placed "upright in a sitting posture" (position)?
10. What is the meaning of: breathing heavily, in his distress, minstrels, his own village, his father's forge, cottage, his misery was interrupted, clumsy hands, an ugly unshaven face, two hairy hands under his armpits?

Language

1. Use these three VERBS in sentences: breathe, heat, cry.

2. ADVERBS

"Redcap was breathing heavily."

The word *heavily* is an adverb, telling us *how* Redcap was breathing.

An ADVERB tells us more about a verb. It adds to a verb, giving more meaning to it, like this:

The boy wrote a sentence. The boy wrote a sentence *hurriedly*.

The adverb *hurriedly* tells us more about the writing. It tells us *how* he wrote.

Think of three adverbs which may be used in (a), three in (b) and three in (c):

(a) The river flows . . . . . .

(b) The girl was working . . . . . .

(c) The man spoke . . . . . .

Here is an example to help you: The boy ran (quickly *or* slowly *or* silently).

Remember: (1) Most adverbs are formed by adding LY to the adjective:
quick, *quickly* A quick answer He ran *quickly*.
(2) With verbs put *adverbs*: She ran slow*ly*.

Form adverbs from these adjectives, then use them in sentences: serious, gay.

3. *Find the Stranger:* ugly unshaven black pretty dirty
4. Use in sentences: lying, laying, quiet, quite.
5. Put into alphabetical order: ugly, unshaven, misery, robbers, upright.
6. Write these sentences correctly:
   (i) My father (writ, written, wrote, write) this letter.
   (ii) The baby had (broke, broken, breaks) the milk jug.
   (iii) The bird (flew, flue, flu, flowed, flown) across the dining-room.
   (iv) This book is (to, two, too) (deer, dear).
   (v) My shoes have just been (sold, soled) and (heeled, healed).
7. Form nouns from these words and prove that they are nouns by seeing if "the" in front makes sense, like this: heavily (adverb): heaviness (noun): "The heaviness of . . .":
   wet, sick, friendly, safe, slept, think, interrupted.
8. Pick out the Proper nouns and write them correctly:
   sarah, monkey, jane, coventry, australia, king, king arthur, mr. johnson, river.
9. What is the plural of son, daughter, handkerchief, echo, calf, witch, goose?

10. Put in punctuation marks and capital letters:
while redcap was searching for red eric he was captured by robbers i fear i shall not see my fathers forge and my own safe bed again he said

11. Make the second pair agree in the same way that the first pair agree:

forge, blacksmith	:	——, porter
parents, children	:	geese, ——
heavy, heavily	:	happy, ——
robbers, steal	:	doctors, ——
minstrels, music	:	postman, ——
village, villagers	:	——, citizens
forgotten, remembered	:	——, sold

12. *Spelling* workers: dent . . . conduc . . .
young ones: go . . ing (goose) . . . net (swan).
Sort out these p . . ces of mat . . . al and sep . . . te the white from the black.
Where have you put the cha . k and the blackb . . . d duster?

13. What are *all* the meanings of sack, pole, forge, lying, ground, back, may?

14. Use in interesting sentences: breathing heavily friendly glow ugly unshaven.

Find Out

1. Find out what these words mean, then use one from each group in sentences:
guess, guessed, guest father, farther, further see, sea some, sum
interrupt, interfere, interest, interval, interview seize, siege, besieged.

2. Find out the meaning of: close at hand, to change hands (2), climb hand over fist, wait on someone hand and foot, given a free hand, have one's hands full (2), hand in glove with someone, hand to hand fighting, heavy-handed, high-handed, lay hands on, take one's life in one's hands, live from hand to mouth, an old hand, out of hand, try one's hand at something, get the upper hand, wash one's hands of it.

3. Think of words which sound the same (or nearly the same) but which are spelt differently: pair, passed, I, vain.
Give the meaning of your words.

4. PLACES OF WORK
A blacksmith works in a *forge*.
Make a list of different kinds of work and say what we call each person's place of work.

9 *Ships and Sharks*

On the 4th May towards midday Méndez noticed a dark triangle in the sea describing sweeping circles around the ship.

Aha! A shark! Méndez had often seen a shark before. Half an hour later there were four sharks circling round the ship. They were even cutting in between the two ships, as if they wanted to have a better look at them from every side.

Other men noticed the sharks too. From the south an impressive shoal of dark triangles came swimming up to the ships and seemed to enjoy performing a dance around them. They were making the wildest leaps.

Porras was the first to say: "That bodes no good."

"They're announcing more hurricanes," said an old sailor.

Columbus pointed to the sky. "It doesn't look like a storm."

The old sailor was obstinate. "Those fellows down there know better," he said. "They don't make mistakes."

"It's another six days to Hispaniola," said the Admiral.

"If only the weather stays as it is," continued the sailor. "These two crocks won't stand up to another hurricane."

"There's no hurricane coming," said Columbus.

Two hours later the school of sharks moved off north-north-westwards, precisely in the direction in which Jahanika lay.

"See that!" cried the Admiral. "They're moving off! Perhaps they'll pay the island of Jahanika a visit now."

From *Son of Columbus* by Hans Baumann

Comprehension

A 1. What was the date and time when Méndez saw the first shark?
2. Where was Méndez?
3. How many sharks were there half-an-hour later?
4. How many ships were there?
5. A large number of sharks came from the (North, South, East, West). Which?
6. The dancers were (sailors, sharks, Méndez and Porras, the Admiral and an old sailor). Which?
7. Who said that the arrival of the sharks was a sign of bad luck?
8. Who was sure that there would not be a storm?
9. How long were the visitors near the ships?
10. What is the meaning of: midday, circles, leaps, hurricanes, island, the school of sharks, pay the island of Jahanika a visit?

B 1. (a) In which direction did the sharks disappear? (b) This direction is nearly (North, South, East, West). Which?
2. How did Méndez know that there was a shark swimming round the ship?
3. At about what time (o'clock) were four sharks swimming round the ships?
4. (a) How many different people speak in the extract?
(b) Who are they?
5. "That *bodes no good*" means: brave and bold, is a bad sign, Illness will follow. Which?
6. (a) What did the arrival of the sharks tell one old sailor? (b) Can you think why he should think this?
7. (a) What did he fear a hurricane might do? (b) Why?
8. (a) Who was as obstinate as the old sailor? (b) How can you tell?
9. At about what time (o'clock) did the sharks swim away?
10. What is the meaning of: a triangle, describing (making) sweeping circles, cutting in, an impressive shoal, announcing, obstinate, Those fellows down there, six days to Hispaniola, precisely?

Language

1. Complete this: Adverbs tell us more about ——. Most adverbs end in —— and tell us —— the action was done.

   Add suitable adverbs to these verbs: were running, shouted, spoke.

   Use one of your phrases in a sentence.

2. COMPARING THINGS: *good, better, best*

   The sharks swam between the ships, as if they wanted a *better* look at them.

   What is the difference between a *good* look, a *better* look, and the *best* look? This is comparing things: one is good, a second is better and a third is the best.

   Do the same with these adjectives:

pretty	——	——	bad	——	——
high	——	——	many	——	——
wet	——	——	little	——	——

   Remember: When you add *er* you are comparing *two* things.
   When you add *est* you are comparing *more than two* things.

   Do NOT say: This is the prettiest of the two dolls.
   Say: This is the prettier of the two dolls.

   Find an *est* word in the Comprehension passage *Ships and Sharks*.

3. Make sense out of these jumbled words: of sailors a one the noticed shark.

4. *Spelling* workers: black . . . . . m . . er young ones: l . . . (sheep) k . . . . . (cat)
   In fairy stor . . . pe . . le can often make themselves inv . . . ble by magic spells.
   Put lab . . . on your raincoats so that you do not lo . . them.

5. Put in alphabetical order: midday, may, men, making, more, make, move.

   Remember: If the first letters are the same, look at the second letters; if the second are the same, look at the third; if the third are the same, look at the fourth, and so on: inter*e*st, inter*r*upt: interE comes before interR, so *interest* comes before *interrupt*.

6. *Find the Stranger:* January Jane June July

7. Make the second pair agree in the same way that the first pair agree:

forest, trees	:	town, ——	doctor, patients	:	teacher, ——
wind, blows	:	fire, ——	late, early	:	slow, ——
drum, drummer	:	piano, ——	hill, mountain	:	wood, ——

8. (a) Give the singular of: circles, men, halves, wolves, handkerchiefs.
   (b) Give the plural of: triangle, hurricane, shoal, child, calf, ox.

9. Write these sentences correctly:
   (i) (Its, It's) a long story.
   (ii) The dog has hurt (its, it's) tail.
   (iii) I hope that the (weather, whether) will stay sunny.
   (iv) Tell me (whether, weather) you like this or not.
   (v) (Hear, Here, Ear) lies the island of Jahanika.
10. Write correctly:
   (i) it is time to go home said my aunt john will go with you
   (ii) robins starlings and sparrows were searching for food
11. What are these places: barracks, a grocery shop, an ice-rink, a stadium, plantation, library, an Art Gallery?
12. Put interesting adjectives in the spaces: The —— sailors had often seen —— sharks before. They believed that the —— arrival of sharks was a —— sign of —— storms but Columbus did not believe such —— tales.
13. What is a verb? Find in the Comprehension passage *Ships and Sharks* (a) three verbs in the Past tense (time) (b) three in the Present tense.
14. Use in interesting sentences: a dark triangle   wildest leaps   the island of Jahanika.

Find Out

1. Find out what these words mean, then use one from each group in sentences:
   perform, inform, reform (2), perfume   pointed (2), appointed, disappointed
   island, isle, islet, highlands, Highlands   weather, whether
   like (2), dislike, alike, unlike   better, butter, batter (2), bitter (2).
2. Find out the meaning of: has seen better days, better late than never, to better oneself, to be better off, think better of it, a change for the better; first come, first served; First Aid, first class, first-rate, on the first floor.
3. Think of words which sound the same (or nearly the same) but which are spelt differently: four, fourth, sea, hour, hours, too, they're, days.
   Give the meaning of your words.
4. SEA EXPLORERS
   (i) Find out all you can about sea explorers like Columbus, Magellan and Vasco da Gama. How did America receive its name?
   (ii) Find out about the tiny size of ocean-going ships of the Middle Ages. Did you know that Columbus' ship "Santa Maria" was smaller than a funnel of the first "Queen Elizabeth"?

10 *Avalanche!*

After we were again in base camp we set out for the North Col. And this time we reached it from two directions—the old way from the East Rongbuk Glacier and a new way from the main Rongbuk Glacier. But we found the new route very steep and even less safe than the old, which was dangerous enough itself. The snow-and-ice slopes below the Col, as I have said, are a place of great avalanche menace, and now for the first time I was caught in one. When it happened there were six of us climbing on two ropes—Captain Oliver, myself, and the Sherpa Wangdi Norbu on one, and Tilman with two Sherpas on the other.

The snow is very steep, and also deep—as high as our waists—and we are moving slowly and with difficulty, when suddenly there is a sort of cracking sound all around us, and the snow begins to move too. The next minute we are all sliding down with it. I am off my feet, turning over and over. My head is under the snow, and it is dark. I remember, of course, what happened here in 1922, and I think, it is the same thing again. It is the end. But at the same time I am struggling, throwing my ice-axe back over my shoulder, trying to stop myself and dig out. And luckily the avalanche stops, and I am not too deep. My axe catches and holds on some solid snow, which allows me to pull myself up. I look around in the bright light, and I am still alive.

From *Man of Everest* by J. R. Ullman

Tenzing, a Sherpa (the name of the people who live near Everest), who climbed Mount Everest with Hillary in 1953, is telling this story about one of his earlier climbs.

Comprehension

A 1. Where did the climbers go when they left camp?

2. A *col* is a dip in a mountain ridge, shaped like a saddle.
   (a) Which was the old way to the North Col? (b) Why was it named North Col?

3. (a) What is a glacier? (b) What was a new way to the North Col?

4. What is an avalanche?

5. How many men were climbing when the avalanche started?

6. Who were fastened together on one rope?

7. Who were on the second rope?

8. How deep was the snow?

9. How often before had Tenzing been in an avalanche?

10. What is the meaning of: we set out for, two directions, new route, dangerous enough, moving slowly and with difficulty, luckily?

B 1. How many Sherpas were climbing? Give their names, if you know them.

2. Tenzing was caught in (a trap, a glacier, a sliding mass of snow, a col). Which?

3. What warning was there of the start of an avalanche?

4. (a) What do you think happened in 1922? (b) What has this to do with it: "It is the end."?

5. What did Tenzing fear was going to happen?

6. What two things saved him?

7. Which was the most dangerous place on the part they were climbing?

8. (a) Did Tenzing die in this avalanche? (b) Can you give two reasons for your answer, one of which is not actually in the extract?

9. Why do you think the story changes *time* halfway through?

10. What is the meaning of: base camp, the main Rongbuk Glacier, a place of great avalanche menace (danger), some solid snow, Man of Everest, "Man of Everest," ice-axe, I am not too deep?

Language

1. Write out three columns: *one* *Comparing two* *Comparing more than two*

one	*Comparing two*	*Comparing more than two*
big	bigger	biggest

Put these words into the first column: old, steep, lucky, thin, then fill in the other two columns.

2. VERBS 2

Is this written in the Present, Past or Future tense (time):

"The snow is very steep, and also deep—as high as our waists—and we are moving slowly and with difficulty, when suddenly there is a sort of cracking sound all around us . . ."?

Change this from the Past to the Present:

We were again in base camp. We reached the glacier from a new direction. We found the new route very steep.

Remember: (1) The verb "to be" (I am, he is, they were, etc.) is not exactly a "doing-word" or action but it is still a verb. You will find it is a helping-word: "I . . . running" needs help before it can make sense: *am*, *was*, etc. help to make sense: I *am* running, I *was* running.

(2) I hope: I am hoping (no *e* before *ing*)

(3) I run: I am running (double letters before *ing*)

Add *ing* to these verbs: pass, race, hit, care, dine, amuse, rip, step, hope, hop, believe, strike, crash, slap.

3. SILENT B: What are these *silent* B words, like *climbing:*

(i) unable to speak (ii) arms and legs (iii) a young sheep (iv) a repairer of burst water-pipes (v) a gravestone (vi) used for tidying the hair (vii) part of the hand (viii) unable to feel because of cold?

4. Put in order, the smallest in height first: hill, hillock, mound, mountain.

5. *Find the Stranger:* glacier snow ropes ice avalanche

6. (a) Think of the opposites of after, North, East, below, first, high, slowly, with difficulty, begins, dark, remember, same, the end, luckily, pull.

(b) Think of words which mean the same as caught, discover, allow, bright, moist.

7. Give the plural of shoulder, ice-axe, myself, difficulty.

8. *Ascent, Ascend; Descent, Descend.*

The nouns end in T, the verbs in D: the ascent, the descent; they ascended, decide to descend.

Use *ascent* and *descend* in sentences. Remember that when you use a verb you may add endings to it, like this: descends, descended.

9. "I remember, of *course*, what happened here in 1922 . . ."
   Use *course* and *coarse* in two sentences.
10. *Spelling* workers: care . . . . . carp . . . . . young ones: duc . . . . . chic . . .
    Please ans . . . my ques . . . . quickly.
    John drop . . . the tin of sa . mon by the ki . . . en door.
11. Put into alphabetical order: axe, avalanche, after, alter, again, against.
12. Put these words into the sentences: from, to, off, of:
    (i) My chair is different —— yours.
    (ii) The careless boy fell —— the swing.
    (iii) I fell out —— the car.
    (iv) We are going —— the Zoo tomorrow.
13. What is an apostrophe? Look in your dictionary, if necessary.
14. Use in interesting sentences: the old way   I was caught   avalanche.

Find Out

1. Find out what these words mean, then use one from each group in sentences: direction, director, direct (2), directory   main, mane   place, plaice   cracking, creaking, crackling, crunching, crinkling, croaking, crouching, crushing   struggling, straggling, stretching, striding, strident, striking (2), stroking, stoking.
2. Find out the meaning of: head over heels, from head to toe, keep or lose one's head, bite someone's head off, a swelled head, a swollen face, cannot make head or tail of it; a watercourse, racecourse, of course.
3. Think of words which sound the same (or nearly the same) but which are spelt differently: for, new, place, caught, waist.
   Give the meaning of your words.
4. MOUNTAINS
   Use reference books, your atlas and the globe to find out where these mountains are: Everest, Ben Nevis, Snowdon, Scafell, Kinder Scout, Fujiyama, the Alps, the Pyrenees, the Pennines, the Andes and the Rocky Mountains.

11

Winter

Sweet blackbird is silenced with chaffinch and thrush,
Only waistcoated robin still chirps in the bush:
Soft sun-loving swallows have mustered in force,
And winged to the spice-teeming southlands their course.

Plump housekeeper dormouse has tucked himself neat,
Just a brown ball in moss with a morsel to eat:
Armed hedgehog has huddled him into the hedge,
While frogs scarce miss freezing deep down in the sedge.

Soft swallows have left us alone in the lurch,
But robin sits whistling to us from his perch:
If I were red robin, I'd pipe you a tune,
Would make you despise all the beauties of June.

But since that cannot be, let us draw round the fire,
Munch chestnuts, tell stories, and stir the blaze higher:
We'll comfort pinched robin with crumbs, little man,
Till he'll sing us the very best song that he can.

Christina Rossetti

Comprehension

A 1. Which season of the year does this poem describe?
2. How many different birds are mentioned?
3. Which animals are mentioned?
4. What looks like a brown ball? Why?
5. How is a blackbird "sweet"?
6. Which birds (a) are silent (b) still sing?
7. (a) How is a hedgehog "armed"? (b) How can a man be armed?
8. What do we do round the fire (in this poem)?
9. Find a kind action in the poem.
10. What is the meaning of: chirps, plump, morsel, huddled, hedge, his perch, pipe you a tune, munch, comfort?

B 1. (a) How is a robin "waistcoated"? (b) Why is this a clever description?
2. If *mustered* means "gathered together" and *winging a course* means "flying away", what is the meaning of lines 3 and 4 in the first verse?
3. Why have the swallows flown away?
4. How can a dormouse be a plump housekeeper?
5. The dormice, hedgehogs and frogs are (fighting, migrating, hibernating, feasting). Which?
6. Why do you think the swallows are called (a) sun-loving (b) soft?
7. What things, besides the title, tell us which season this is?
8. Write down any three "beauties of June" which you like.
9. Why is the robin "pinched"?
10. What is the meaning of: is silenced, mustered in force, spice-teeming, a morsel to eat, huddled him into the hedge, scarce miss freezing, sedge, left us alone in the lurch, despise, stir the blaze higher?

Language

1. Change these verbs to the Present time, like came, COME (I *come* early every day.): began, blew, chose, have broken, clung, drew, drove, fought, have forgotten, froze, have written, did.

2. WHO OWNS IT ?

the robin's waistcoat

The "high comma" is called an APOSTROPHE.

It tells us who is the OWNER of something or to whom something belongs:

The robin's waistcoat: the waistcoat of the robin (belonging to the robin)

Remember: Rules about the position of the apostrophe:

(1) Singular owner: add *'s* one cat: the cat's milk

(2) Plural owner ending in S: add ' two cats: the cats' milk

(3) Plural owner not ending in S: add *'s* men: the men's coats

To check that you have not made a mistake, ask "Who is the owner?" and put the apostrophe straight after that word, like this:

The mans clothes. Who is the owner? The man. Put the apostrophe after MAN: The man's clothes.

Put in the apostrophe and *check* that it is in the correct place:

our cats milk (one cat), both cats milk, a mans clothes, mens clothes, a girls school (hundreds of girls), a womans handbag, womens magazines, a childs toys, childrens toys, a wolfs cubs, the geeses dinner, lambs tails.

Write two sentences, one containing the word *fox's*, the other *rats'*.

3. What is the plural of: dormouse, thrush, bush, brook, cry, child?

What is the singular of: deer, lambs, cuffs, knaves, knives, noises?

4. Write this correctly:

We (past, passed) the tree twice without noticing the squirrel but the third time we went (past, passed) we saw it.

5. Put these in their proper order, the smallest in size, value, etc. first:

county, city, village, town, country.

grey, white, black, brown.

50p, 1p, 10p, 5p.

cool, cold, freezing, tepid, boiling, hot.

elephant, dog, lion, mouse, fly.

brook, ocean, sea, spring, river.

6. *Find the Stranger:* bush village hedge gorse tree

7. (a) Which words in the poem rhyme with bush, force, fire, perch?

(b) Which of these words rhymes with *seize*: size, breeze, siege, sieve?

8. Put into alphabetical order: robin, swallow, bush, brook, fern, fox, frog, frock

9. Find the missing words:

Family	*Father*	*Mother*	*Young*	*Home*	*Group*
deer	——	——	——	parks	a —— of deer
——	——	——	lamb	——	a —— (2) of sheep

10. Write correctly:
    (i) why do you like to wander about the countryside in all kinds of weather i asked the old tramp
    (ii) christina rossetti wrote a poem called winter
    (iii) stop shouted the farmer angrily to the two boys where do you think youre going dont you know this is private property
11. Think of words which mean the same, or nearly the same, as sweet, under, broad, halt, brook, chirps, large, silent, night, joy.
12. Describe these colours: brown, mauve, crimson, scarlet, violet, fawn, purple.
13. *Spelling* workers: sh . . . erd doc . . .
    young ones: ca . . (cattle) cat . . pil . . . (butterfly)
    Marilyn res . . bles her mother (looks like her).
    Jill is a gra . . ful dancer who has pract . . . d hard for many years.
14. Use in interesting sentences: a brown ball freezing the beauties of June.

Find Out

1. Find out what these words mean, then use one from each group in sentences:
   thrush, brush, crush, hush, push, rush, thrust, trust course, coarse
   flying, fleeing, fledgling, fleeting, flickering, flitting, flocking, flogging
   chattering, shattering, clattering, chatting, clamouring, clambering, shambling
   road, rode, rowed where, were, wear not, knot one, won.
2. Find out the meaning of: do your best, make the best of it, as good as gold, Good Friday, in a good humour, a Good Samaritan, a goods train; man-hole, a man of his word, man the boats, as one man, clergyman.
3. Think of words which sound the same (or nearly the same) but which are spelt differently: teem, their, course, red, night, beat, past.
   Give the meaning of your words.
4. BIRDS
   Find out about (a) British birds (b) Foreign birds.
   What is the meaning of migration, resident British birds, summer or winter migrants, aviaries, rookeries, birds of prey, eyries, owlets, cygnets, fowls?

12 *Binning's Trick*

The castle of Linlithgow was in the hands of the English, but it was won from them by the help of a poor farmer called Binning.

The castle was very strong. It was surrounded by a loch, and a moat crossed by a drawbridge. Under the archway of the entrance there was a portcullis.

It seemed hopeless to attempt to take the castle, it was so strong.

One day the English Governor ordered Binning to bring a cart-load of hay to the castle, as he was in need of some for his horses. Binning promised to bring it, but he made up his mind to take the castle at the same time. Quickly and quietly his plans were made. During the night some Scottish soldiers crept as near to the castle walls as they dared, and hid where they could not be seen by the English. Then very early in the morning Binning loaded his cart. But he did not load it with hay only. In the cart lay eight strong men, clad in steel, and armed with swords and battle-axes. Over these men, so as quite to cover them, Binning placed a light load of hay.

He then harnessed his oxen with ropes to the heavy cart, and set out for the castle. A servant sat in front, driving, and Binning himself walked by the side of the cart, with a stick in his hand and his woodman's axe at his belt.

From *Scotland's Story* by H. E. Marshall

Comprehension

A 1. Where was the castle?
2. What was the farmer's name?
3. Why did it seem hopeless to try to capture the castle?
4. (a) Who wanted some hay? (b) Why?
5. Why did he ask Binning for it?
6. How did Binning make his plans: rapidly, slowly, loudly, noisily, secretly?
7. What did Scottish soldiers do during darkness?
8. When did Binning load his cart?
9. Who had (a) battle-axes (b) a woodman's axe (c) a servant?
10. What is the meaning of: surrounded by, a moat, drawbridge, entrance, hopeless, ordered, a cart-load of hay, a light load, oxen?

B 1. (a) What had the English captured? (b) From whom? (c) Can you think of the reason why?
2. (a) Describe the castle of Linlithgow. (b) In which country was it?
3. What do you think was the work of the English Governor?
4. (a) What did Binning determine to do? (b) Can you guess why?
5. (a) What did he load into his cart? (b) Why did he have a light load of hay?
6. On the way to the castle, who or what (a) drove (b) pulled (c) walked (d) rode?
7. How do you think Binning hoped to capture the castle?
8. How do we know that he was successful?
9. Think of several reasons why this story cannot be about modern times (today).
10. What is the meaning of: a loch, portcullis, to attempt, as near as they dared, clad in steel, armed with, so as quite to cover them, harnessed, at his belt, in the hands of?

Language

1. Put in the apostrophe:

(i) Binnings stick was in his hand and his woodmans axe was at his belt.
(ii) The Ladies Club meets on Thursday evenings.

2. INDIRECT SPEECH

In Exercise 2 we talked about Direct Speech (the exact words spoken, inside inverted commas).

If we do *not* have the exact words spoken, we do *not* use inverted commas:

One day the English Governor ordered Binning to bring a cart-load of hay.

Remember: (1) When we do NOT have the exact words spoken, we call it INDIRECT SPEECH.

(2) Indirect Speech is also called REPORTED SPEECH, because someone is reporting or telling us what was said, without giving us the exact words spoken.

Change from Indirect to Direct Speech:

Binning told the eight soldiers that he would cover them over with hay.

Change from Direct to Indirect Speech:

"I'll bring a cart-load of hay to the castle in the morning," said Binning.

3. What are the opposites of hopeless, won, poor, strong, ordered, bring, quickly, near, quietly, night, early, light (2)?

4. *Find the Stranger:* axe battle-axe castle sword dagger

5. ". . . ordered Binning to *bring* a cart-load of hay."

Remember: You BRING something with you. You go to FETCH something.

What is the difference in meaning here?

(a) My father promised to fetch some paraffin later in the week.

(b) My father promised to bring some paraffin later in the week.

Use *bring* and *fetch* in two sentences.

6. The English *Governor* of Linlithgow.

What words ending in OR have these meanings: (1) he betrays his country (begins with t) (2) he invents (i) (3) rescued after a shipwreck (s) (4) he inspects (i) (5) competes in races (c) (6) writes books (a) (7) comes to see you (v) (8) an Army officer (m) (9) he decorates rooms with paint and wallpaper (d) (10) a seaman (s)?

7. Use *light* in four sentences: (a) and (b) as adjectives (c) as a noun (d) as a verb.

8. *Spelling* shopkeepers: c . . mist gro . . . bu . . . er gr . . . gro . . .

sounds: w . is . . ing w . ir . ing

I am not sat . . . ied with your behav . . . r, John. You sho . . d be ash . . ed.

9. Write correctly:
   (i) The English sentries could not see (anyone, nobody).
   (ii) The Governor could not wait (no, any) longer for the hay.
   (iii) I cannot write (no, any) faster.

10. Pick out the three adverbs and use them in sentences: quickly, brave, quietly, hot, strong, helpful, slow, carelessly.

11. Say which proverb best fits the story "Binning's Trick", then say why it fits:
    When the cat's away, the mice will play. New brooms sweep clean.
    Too many cooks spoil the broth. Where there's a will, there's a way.

12. (a) What games are played on courts, greens, pitches?
    (b) What are these places: zoological gardens, aviaries, restaurants, colleges, laundries, orchards, cinemas, museums, docks, shipyards, reservoirs?

13. Put suitable joining-words into these sentences:
    (i) —— sealing the envelope, I remembered something which I had left out of my letter, —— I had to open it again.
    (ii) —— John —— Peter can play in the final tomorrow —— they are ill.

14. Use in interesting sentences: The castle of Linlithgow   under the archway   eight strong men.

Find Out

1. Find out what these words mean, then use one from each group in sentences:
   drawbridge, drawback, drawer, drawl, draught (2)   horse, hoarse
   nightfall, nightingale, nightmare   a light, alight   hoard, horde
   lighten (2), lightening, lightning.

2. Find out the meaning of: to mind your p's and q's, bear in mind, change one's mind, have a good mind to do something, make up one's mind, speak one's mind, mind the baby, Mind that bull!; out of sight, out of mind; absent-minded, Two minds with but a single thought.

3. Think of words which sound the same (or nearly the same) but which are spelt differently: won, loch, to, load, need, horse, made, eight, steel.
   Give the meaning of your words.

4. SCOTLAND
   Find out about the following: the Highlands, the Lowlands, the River Clyde, the Hebrides, Ben Nevis, John o' Groats, Bonnie Prince Charlie, the thistle, the Flying Scotsman and the Forth Bridge.

13

A Storm at Sea

The storm was so violent, that I saw what is not often seen, the master, the boatswain, and some others more sensible than the rest, at their prayers, and expecting every moment when the ship would go to the bottom.

In the middle of the night, and under all the rest of our distresses, one of the men that had been down on purpose to see, cried out we had sprung a leak; another said there was four foot of water in the hold. Then all hands were called to the pump. At that very word my heart, as I thought, died within me, and I fell backwards upon the side of my bed where I sat, into the cabin. However, the men roused me, and told me, that I that was able to do nothing before, was as well able to pump as another; at which I stirred up and went to the pump and worked very heartily.

While this was doing, the master, seeing some light colliers, who, not able to ride out the storm, were obliged to slip and run away to sea, and would come near us, ordered to fire a gun as a signal of distress. I who knew nothing what that meant, was so surprised, that I thought the ship had broken, or some dreadful thing had happened. In a word, I was so surprised, that I fell down in a swoon. As this was a time when every-body had his own life to think of, nobody minded me, or what was become of me; but another man stepped up to the pump, and thrusting me aside with his foot, let me lie, thinking I was dead; and it was a great while before I came to myself.

From *Robinson Crusoe* by Daniel Defoe

Comprehension

A 1. What was fierce?

2. (a) Who prayed? (b) Why?
3. (a) When was a leak discovered? (b) Who found it?
4. How deep was the water inside the ship's hull?
5. Why did Robinson Crusoe fall?
6. Why did the others make him stand again?
7. What was the signal that they needed help?
8. Why did Robinson Crusoe think that the ship was wrecked?
9. (a) Did anyone help him when he fainted? (b) What tells you?
10. What is the meaning of: violent, sensible, on purpose to see, cried out, the hold, roused me, stirred up, some dreadful thing, let me lie?

B 1. What sensible action was taken?

2. "Then all hands were called to the pump." What does this mean?
3. (a) What is another name for the "master" in this story? (b) Which other kinds of master do you know?
4. "Colliers" is a word which has two different meanings, one being men who work in a *coal mine*. What do you think "colliers" are in this story?
5. Why did they run away to sea?
6. Why did Robinson Crusoe faint?
7. (a) Was he a good sailor? (b) How do you know?
8. Why did nobody worry about him?
9. Rewrite in modern English: (a) I that was able to do nothing before (b) ordered to fire a gun (c) I who knew nothing what that meant (d) expecting every moment when the ship would go to the bottom (e) While this was doing.
10. What is the meaning of: boatswain, our distresses, had sprung a leak, died within me, worked very heartily, light colliers, ride out the storm, obliged to slip (had to slip), in a swoon, nobody minded me, a great while?

Language

1. Change to Indirect Speech (*not* the exact words spoken):
   (i) "Captain," said Robinson Crusoe in a panic, "I'm afraid of this storm. I've never been to sea before. I'm not used to it."
   (ii) "You'll see worse storms than this," replied the captain.

2. Explain the difference in meaning between these two requests:
   Fetch some more coal for the fire, please.
   Bring some more coal for the fire, please.

3. VERBS 3
   In Exercise 10 we talked about actions in the PRESENT tense or time: I run, I am running.
   When the action took place in the PAST, we can say: I was running, I ran, I have run, I had run.
   Remember: (1) Simple or ordinary PAST: ran, came, wrote, took
   (2) PAST with *have*, *has* or *had*: have run, has come, had written, have taken.
   Choose the correct word from those in the brackets:
   (i) We have (beat, beaten) all the other teams at football.
   (ii) When the ship (sunk, sank) the sailors (swum, swam) to the shore.
   (iii) The girls (began, begun) netball yesterday.
   (iv) The gale has (blew, blown, blow) down our elm-tree.
   (v) My sister has just (broke, broken) a vase.
   (vi) I (knew, known) that he (did, done) it.

4. Make the second pair agree in the same way that the first pair agree:

beautiful, ugly	:	correct, ——
calf, calves	:	child, ——
man, woman	:	——, spinster
sad, happy	:	possible, ——
arm, fingers	:	leg, ——
king, palace	:	——, igloo
cat, kitten	:	——, cygnet

5. Use these words in sentences: thought, though, through, threw, throughout.

6. What is the difference between a cinema, a theatre and a concert hall?

7. What work is done by a helmsman, steward, magistrate, blacksmith, caretaker, carpenter, navvy, drover, driver (several), an engineer (several)?

8. *Find the Stranger:* boatswain stoker colliery engineer gamekeeper docker

9. Think of suitable nouns to fit these adjectives, like this: fierce *wolf*:
faithful, cunning, stubborn, enormous, dangerous, ferocious.

10. (a) Give the singular of distresses, men, neighbours, two pairs of scissors.
(b) Give the plural of fairy, collier, colliery, valley, knife, calf.

11. Put in the apostrophe:
(i) the ships timbers (one ship) (ii) ships timbers (many ships)
(iii) Daniel Defoes book (iv) sailors hammocks (v) lions manes

12. *Spelling* From their first three letters, spell the words which have these meanings:
(a) of no value (wor) (b) take prisoner (cap) (c) remove the wrapper (unw) (d) slightly wet (moi) (e) dear, costly (exp) (f) give in (yie) (g) A German is a for——. (h) The station at the end of a railway line (ter).

13. Change the following verbs so that they end in *ing*:
come, slip, ride, name, run, swim, catch, fly, flee, race, lose, begin.

14. Use in interesting sentences: a violent storm fell backwards away to sea.

Find Out

1. Find out what these words mean, then use one from each group in sentences:
violent, violet, violin, violinist heart, hearth, heartless
sensible, senseless (2), sensation (2), sentence (2), sentry, sensitive
backwards, backwoods thrust, thrush, trust expect, except, expert, accept.

2. Find out the meaning of: Come along!; easy come, easy go; come off badly or second-best, come what may, to come about, to come to pass, still to come, to come across something, come down heavily on someone, come off scot-free, come round (2), come to blows, come to harm, come up smiling, come into a fortune, come to nothing, It now comes back to me.

3. Think of words which sound the same (or nearly the same) but which are spelt differently: more, our, leak, died, stirred, knew, while.
Give the meaning of your words.

4. OCEANS
Use atlas and globe to find the five oceans of the world.
Which oceans wash the shores of Ireland, Cornwall, Australia, Ceylon, Japan, North Russia, Canada, Brazil, Africa and Scotland?

14 *Searching for Tom*

For good Sir John had slept very badly that night; and he said to his lady: "My dear, the boy must have got over into the grouse-moors, and lost himself; and he lies very heavily on my conscience, poor little lad. But I know what I will do."

So, at five the next morning up he got, and into his bath, and into his shooting-jacket and gaiters, and into the stable-yard, like a fine old English gentleman, with a face as red as a rose, and a hand as hard as a table, and a back as broad as a bullock's; and bade them bring his shooting pony, and the keeper to come on his pony, and the huntsman, and the first whip, and the second whip, and the under-keeper with the bloodhound in a leash—a great dog as tall as a calf, of the colour of a gravel walk, with mahogany ears and nose, and a throat like a church bell. They took him up to the place where Tom had gone into the wood; and there the hound lifted up his mighty voice and told them all he knew.

Then he took them to the place where Tom had climbed the wall; and they shoved it down, and all got through.

And then the wise dog took them over the moor, and over the fells, step by step, very slowly; for the scent was a day old, you know, and very light from the heat and drought. But that was why cunning old Sir John started at five in the morning.

And at last he came to the top of Lewthwaite Crag, and there he bayed, and looked up in their faces as much as to say, "I tell you he is gone down here!"

From *The Water Babies* by Charles Kingsley

Comprehension

A 1. To whom did Sir John speak? (What *relation* was she?)

2. What was the name of the boy who had gone across the moorland?
3. The following morning, Sir John arose (late, early, very early, at his usual time). Which?
4. What did he do before dressing?
5. What was (a) red (b) hard (c) broad (d) tall?
6. How did Sir John travel in pursuit of the lost boy?
7. "In a leash" means "on a lead". Why was the dog not free?
8. What do you think an under-keeper is?
9. What do you think the dog told them when he "lifted up his mighty voice"?
10. What is the meaning of: a bloodhound, a calf, a gravel walk, a church bell, shoved it down, step by step, cunning, bayed?

B 1. Why had Sir John slept badly?

2. What did he mean by: ". . . he lies very heavily on my conscience", if the word *conscience* means "knowing right from wrong"?
3. Why do you think Sir John wore his shooting-jacket and gaiters?
4. (a) Who went with him? (b) What went with them? (c) Why?
5. Why was Sir John wise to start out very early in the morning?
6. What work do you think these men did: (a) the first whip (b) the second whip?
7. What ordinary colours (black, white, brown, etc.) do you think the dog was?
8. How could its throat be like a church bell?
9. Why did they push the wall down? They must have had a special reason.
10. What is the meaning of: good Sir John, grouse-moors, like a fine old English gentleman, a bullock, his shooting pony, mahogany, fells, the scent, very light from the heat . . ., drought, Lewthwaite Crag?

Language

1. Fill in the missing words:

Present	*Simple Past*	*Past with "have, has or had"*
he lies very heavily	he	he has . . . .
I know	I.	I have . . . .
I do	I	I have . . . .

2. AS RED AS A ROSE

We use sayings like that to describe things vividly. If we are cold, it is more vivid to say "I feel as cold as ice . . ." than to say "I feel cold . . .".

Complete these sayings: as busy as ——, as cunning as ——, as dull as ——, as gentle as ——, as heavy as ——, as poor as ——, as proud as ——.

Remember: Sayings like *as red as a rose* are called SIMILES because they say that something is similar to (like) something else.

3. ". . . the boy must have *got* over . . . up he *got* . . . all *got* through . . ."

Do not use the lazy word *got*. It is a very dull and boring word. Think of interesting words instead of *got* (and *get*). Think *how* it happened, like this: *I got the bus to school: how* did you *get* the bus? Did you stroll down the street, run, race, dawdle, hurry, dash, hop, skip, walk?

Rewrite these three parts of the story about Tom, without using *got*:

(i) So at five in the morning up he got. (ii) The boy must have got over into the grouse-moors. (iii) They shoved it down and all got through.

4. Change to Direct Speech (the exact words spoken):

Sir John told his head gamekeeper to bring the bloodhound to help in the search.

Change to Indirect Speech:

Sir John said to his wife, "The boy must have gone over into the grouse-moors and lost his way."

5. *Find the Stranger:* Sir John Tom lady huntsman keeper

6. "For *good* Sir John had slept very *badly* that night . . ."

Be careful with the adjectives: good, bad; and the adverbs: well, badly.

Do *not* say: You work very *good. How* you work is an adverb: You work very *well.*

Write these correctly:

(i) The children were praised because they spoke (good, well, bad, badly).
(ii) The villain behaved very (good, well, bad, badly).
(iii) The vicar was a (well, good), kind man.

7. ALL ARE WHAT ? Say what they all are on each line:

calf, bloodhound, pony, dog, bullock
crash, bang, roar, whine, buzz, hum
robin, wren, jackdaw, cuckoo, raven, falcon
carnation, rhododendron, chrysanthemum, dahlia, daffodil
house, mansion, flat, bungalow, cottage
measles, pneumonia, chicken-pox, influenza

8. Think of words which mean the same or nearly the same as these words: the *next* morning, jacket, as red as a rose, a *broad* river, a very large wood, lifted up, shoved, wise, slowly, cunning, at last, the mountain *top*.
9. Use these words (pronouns) in sentences: who, whom, which, whose.
10. Give the plural of: lady, boy, gentleman, pony, calf, huntsman, he, potato.
11. What are *all* the meanings of lies, rose, yard, calf, light, dear, step, hard?
12. *Spelling* sounds: scr . . . ing squ . . . ing (2) bu . . ing swi . . ing
    Be pun . . . . ., not late. The poor kitten was fri . . . ened by the dog.
    Sir Francis Drake f . . . . t ag . . . st the Spaniards.
13. What are the opposites of kind, enemy, satisfied, ascended, black, ended?
14. What do these two words mean: male and female?
15. Use in interesting sentences: next morning Lewthwaite Crag a church bell.

Find Out

1. Find out what these words mean, then use one from each group in sentences:
    hard (2), hardy, hardly jacket, jackal, jack (2), jackdaw
    broad, breadth, brood (2), braid, bride, bridal, bridle, bridegroom
    whip, whippet, whisper, whirl, whisk, whirr, whimper, whine, whizz.
2. Find out the meaning of: behind someone's back, go back on one's word, a back number (of a magazine), to back out, take a back seat, turn one's back, to back up, put someone's back up, backs to the wall, to back a vehicle; to bring to light, as light as —— (3), light-fingered, light-headed, light-hearted, make light of something, a light meal, throw light on a problem, a light sleeper, like greased lightning, His face lit up.
3. Think of words which sound the same (or nearly the same) but which are spelt differently: great, nose, him, moor, scent.

    Give the meaning of your words.
4. DOGS

    What do these dogs look like: Alsatians, collies, dachshunds, retrievers, Pekinese, pointers, greyhounds, foxhounds, spaniels, bulldogs?

    Have they any special use? How did they receive their names?

15

Magic Music

Into the street the Piper stept,
   Smiling first a little smile,
As if he knew what magic slept
   In his quiet pipe the while;
Then, like a musical adept,
To blow the pipe his lips he wrinkled,
And green and blue his sharp eyes twinkled,
Like a candle flame where salt is sprinkled;
And ere three shrill notes the pipe uttered,
You heard as if an army muttered;
And the muttering grew to a grumbling,
And the grumbling grew to a mighty rumbling;
And out of the houses the rats came tumbling;
Great rats, small rats, lean rats, brawny rats,
Brown rats, black rats, grey rats, tawny rats,
Grave old plodders, gay young friskers,
   Fathers, mothers, uncles, cousins,
Cocking tails and pricking whiskers,
   Families by tens and dozens,
Brothers, sisters, husbands, wives—
Followed the Piper for their lives.

. . . .

Once more he stept into the street,
   And to his lips again
Laid his long pipe of smooth straight cane;
And ere he blew three notes (such sweet
Soft notes as yet musician's cunning
   Never gave the enraptured air)
There was a rustling, that seemed like a bustling
Of merry crowds justling at pitching and hustling,
Small feet were pattering, wooden shoes clattering,
Little hands clapping, and little tongues chattering,
And, like fowls in a farmyard when barley is scattering
Out came the children running. . . .

From *The Pied Piper of Hamelin* by Robert Browning

Comprehension

A 1. (a) What is a piper? (b) Why do you think he was called the Pied Piper?
2. Why was he smiling?
3. Why did he wrinkle his lips?
4. (a) What shone green and blue? (b) Think of two more things, one green, one blue, not in the poem-extract.
5. (a) Did the piper sprinkle salt on a candle flame? (b) How do you know?
6. (a) What rushed out of the houses of Hamelin? (b) Who rushed out?
7. Where did the rats go?
8. What made these noises: (a) clatter (b) patter (c) clapping (d) chattering?
9. Why are fowls mentioned?
10. What is the meaning of: shrill, muttering, grumbling, rumbling, tumbling, smooth, straight, rustling, pattering, clattering, clapping, chattering?

B 1. (a) How would you spell "stept"? (b) Why do you think it is spelt "stept" here?
2. What magic "slept in his quiet pipe"?
3. How can we tell that the magic worked quickly?
4. How do we know that there was a multitude of rats?
5. (a) Did the piper play different music for the children? (b) How do you know?
6. Find a word in the extract which means a very clever person, an expert.
7. How could the children run out like fowls?
8. (a) Make a list of the adjectives describing the rats.
(b) Give each adjective a different noun of your own.
9. In the first part of the extract the Pied Piper helps the Hamelin people. Then they refuse to pay him. What is their punishment for broken promises?
10. What is the meaning of: slept in his quiet pipe the while, the pipe uttered, brawny rats, tawny rats, grave old plodders, gay young friskers, musician's cunning, enraptured air (*rapture* means great joy), for their lives, wrinkled, twinkled, sprinkled, bustling?

Language

1. Complete these similes:
as brave as ——, as changeable as ——, as clear as ——, as sound as ——, as —— as a daisy, as —— as the hills, as —— as an eel, as —— as a doornail.

2. MALE and FEMALE

"Fathers, mothers, uncles . . . brothers, sisters, husbands, wives . . ."
Make two columns, *male* and *female*, putting all those words into the proper column.

Remember: We call *male* words *masculine*, *female* words *feminine*.

Give the feminine of lion, dog-fox, actor, bridegroom, king, hero.
Give the masculine of cow, goose, duck, duchess, spinster, princess.

3. What creatures or things might make these noises: patter, rustle, clatter, clap, chatter, squeak, jingle, crackle, bubble, rattle?

4. *Spelling* Spell the names of these buildings:
(1) a king's home (pal . . .) (2) Its light warns sailors of danger (li . . . house)
(3) a horse's home (sta . . .) (4) a house with no upstair rooms (bun . . . . .)
(5) We see films here (cin . . .) (6) an aeroplane-shed (han . . .)
(7) a large storehouse (war . . . . . .) (8) a very big work-place (fac. . . .)

5. "*Into* the street the Piper stept . . ."
Note the difference between *in* and *into*. What is the difference in meaning here:

He ran *in* the room.	He ran *into* the room.
He dived *in* the pool.	He dived *into* the pool.
He climbed *in* the gym.	He climbed *into* the gym.?

Sometimes, using the wrong word makes nonsense:
He burst into the room. (rushed into it) He burst *in* the room. (Nonsense)

6. ". . . the *enraptured* air . . ."
When we put *en* at the front of the noun *rapture* (great joy or delight), we form the *verb* "to enrapture" which means "to fill with delight". Sometimes we add *en* to the end of a word (*n* if it ends in *e*) to form the *verb*, like fright, frighten.

Put *en* at the front or end of these words to make verbs: sweet, deep, large, rage, strength, loose, wide, bright.

7. Put into alphabetical order: street, smile, step, sharp, salt, small.

8. Use these words in sentences: magician, musician.

9. Write correctly: the pied piper of hamelin is the title of a long poem by robert browning who also wrote the poem with the long title how they brought the good news from ghent to aix

10. Think of the opposites of smiling, quiet, long, smooth, straight, merry, rosy.

11. *Find the Stranger:* father uncle brother mother husband

12. (a) Which words in the poem rhyme with smile, uttered, friskers, cane?
(b) Which of these words rhymes with *vein*: pine, view, foreign, reign?

13. Make the second pair agree in the same way that the first pair agree:

rat, animal	:	robin, ——
fowls, farmyard	:	——, garage
feet, pattering	:	——, clapping
apples, fruit	:	cabbages, ——
king, palace	:	——, warren
uncle, aunt	:	——, niece
hammer, nails	:	——, screws
tree, trunk	:	flower, ——

14. Write correctly:
(i) (Them, Those) apples (are, is) not ripe.
(ii) I like (that, those) kind of book.
(iii) I (beat, won) him in the boxing match.
(iv) John fell (off, of) the tree.
(v) The thunder roared, the (lightening, lightning) flashed.

15. Use in interesting sentences: green and blue   a mighty rumbling   rustling.

Find Out

1. Find out what these words mean, then use one from each group in sentences:
flame, flare, flake   family, familiar, famine, famished, famous
army, arms (2), armour, armada, armful, harmful, harmless   you, yew, ewe
shrill, thrill, trill, rill   has laid, has lain.

2. Find out the meaning of: all along, all the better, All Fools' Day, to be all ears, to be all eyes, on all-fours, go all out, an all-rounder, all and sundry; give blow for blow, come to blows, It's an ill wind that blows nobody any good.

3. Think of words which sound the same (or nearly the same) but which are spelt differently: fowls, boys, tails, knew, blue, where.
Give the meaning of your words.

4. RATS and MICE
What are rodents? What are "water rats"? Why are rats dangerous? Which two types are found in our country? How did rats spread plague?

16 *The Fishing Fleet's Return*

A small group of men stood at the high sea-walls of the town, their hands shading their eyes as they looked westward toward the Atlantic. Above them sea-gulls wheeled and glided on their endless flights across the water-front. Below them the waters of the English Channel washed lightly against the face of the huge granite rock the town was built on. At other times these men had seen the tides sweep in from the Atlantic, pound heavily against the ramparts of rock and wall, and leap high over them to splash down the streets of the town. But today the waters were only slapping playfully against the ancient rock. Today the old sea-port sat quietly in the late summer sun.

Suddenly one of the men pointed out to sea and shouted, "A sail! A sail!"

The others near him picked up the cry and in a moment it was being echoed by dozens of voices within the town.

"A sail! A sail!"

"The fishing-boats are coming in!"

"The men are home again."

As if by magic people appeared from all parts of the town. They hurried through the winding, narrow streets to the look-out points and were soon peering anxiously toward the sails growing larger in the west.

From *Man from St. Malo* by R. D. Ferguson

Comprehension

A 1. Who stood on the sea-walls?
2. In which direction were they looking: North, South, East or West?
3. What did the town stand on?
4. What would the men see if they looked (a) upwards (b) downwards?
5. (a) Was the sea rough? (b) How do you know?
6. (a) Who or what was being slapped? (b) Why?
7. (a) Who saw something? (b) What did he see?
8. Why was everyone suddenly excited?
9. How could the sails grow larger?
10. What is the meaning of: sea-walls, wheeled and glided, the water-front, washed lightly against, slapping playfully, tides, As if by magic?

B 1. (a) Why did the men shade their eyes? (b) What time of day do you think it was? (c) How does the answer to the first part of this question tell you the time of day?
2. What are the English Channel and the Atlantic?
3. (a) What sometimes splashed into the town? (b) When?
4. How can people pick up a cry?
5. Why do you think the people were "soon peering anxiously"?
6. How can we tell that people *suddenly poured out* of the town?
7. (a) Think of two meanings for "the late summer sun". (b) Which of those two meanings fits this passage?
8. The fishermen have been away for a long time. How can we tell this?
9. (a) In which two countries might this old sea-port be? (b) What are the clues which help you?
10. What is the meaning of: endless flights, the face of the huge granite rock, At other times, pound heavily against the ramparts of rock, ancient rock, being echoed, look-out points?

Language

1. Say whether these words are masculine or feminine:
a small group of men, lions, a fierce vixen, a noisy goose, a nervous boy, my polite nephew, the hero, a wild stallion, a tigress.

2. GROUPS OF COLLECTIONS

"A small *group* of men stood at the high sea-walls . . ."

What do we call a group or collection of people watching a match, in church or chapel, at the theatre, crowding the streets on market day (a crowd or ——)?

Complete these "collections" or groups (some may have more than one answer):

(a) *Living:* a litter of ——, a crew of ——, a herd or drove of —— (difference?), a flock of ——, a —— of thieves, a —— of wolves, a shoal of ——.

(b) *Not living:* a —— of flowers, a —— of books, a suit of ——, a suite of ——, a tuft of ——, a bundle of ——, a clump of ——, a —— of ships.

3. *Find the Stranger:* men people seagulls fishermen sailors

4. Choose the words which fit:

The (old, ancient, antique) men stared (anxiously, jokingly, foolishly) out to sea, afraid that the fishing fleet had been (sank, sunk, sinking) in the fierce storm.

5. (a) Complete this table of comparisons (comparing things):

high sea-walls	higher sea-walls	the highest sea-walls
a small group	——	——
old sea-port	——	——
late	——	——
narrow streets	——	——

(b) Complete this by putting *tall, taller* or *tallest* in the gaps:

There were two —— strangers on my doorstep. The —— one spoke first.

6. *Spelling* our body: sho . . . er an . . . s f . . . head mus . . . s

Are you stop . . . . for the football prac . . . . at four o'clock?

A m . ster . . . s stranger called at the p . . . . . -station.

7. Write these sentences correctly:

(i) The fishing boats sailed (straight, strait) (through, threw) the narrow channel.

(ii) The (buoy, boy) has (fell, fallen, fall) off the (key, quay).

(iii) My (farther, father) is a fisherman.

8. Pick out the four adverbs, then use one of them in a sentence:

lightly, slow, naughty, heavy, heavily, playfully, kitten, quietly.

9. Put in the missing words:

(a) Our new car is different —— the old one.

(b) Are you sure —— the answer?

(c) The farmer was angry —— the trespassers.

(d) He fell —— the wall —— the sea.

10. Change this sentence to (a) the Present tense (time) (b) the Simple Past (like *ran*):

The townsfolk had often seen the tides sweep in from the Atlantic Ocean.

11. Which word fits?

(1) The men are waiting for the *coming* of the boats. (departure, arrival)

(2) He wrote the message in his *daily notebook*. (diary, dairy)

(3) Our teacher's voice was *husky* today. (horse, hoarse)

12. Put into alphabetical order: men, man, magic, wall, town, sun.

13. Make the second pair agree in the same way that the first pair agree:

snow, white	:	coal, ——
soldier, army	:	sailor, ——
John, Smith	:	Christian name or forename, ——
snowdrop, white	:	poppy, ——
arm, hand	:	leg, ——

14. (a) What is a sentence? (b) What is a paragraph? (c) What is a phrase?

15. Use in interesting sentences: a small group of   wheeled and glided
huge granite rock   pound heavily.

Find Out

1. Find out what these words mean, then use one from each group in sentences:
channel, The English Channel, canal   tide, tidings, tidily
seaport, support, suppose, sufficient, suffocate, surprise, surround, surrender
narrow, harrow, barrow (2), burrow, borrow   appear, a pear, a pair.

2. Find out the meaning of: time and again, for the time being, to pass the time of day, Old Father Time, to keep good time, time hangs heavily, the time of one's life, in next to no time, on time, no time like the present, just in time, in good time, time after time, from time to time, Time and tide wait for no man.

3. Think of words which sound the same (or nearly the same) but which are spelt differently: sun, sail, peer, sea, their, in, were.
Give the meaning of your words.

4. FISHING
Find out about drifters and trawlers.
Find in your atlas: Grimsby, Hull, Aberdeen, Lowestoft, Fleetwood, Great Yarmouth, Lerwick, Leith, the Dogger Bank and Iceland.

17 *Out at Night*

He felt safer when he reached the bottom of the stairs. He unlocked the back door, holding the key with both hands to steady its turn. He had to stand on one of the kitchen chairs to reach the top bolt; then he was outside in the moonlight.

He looked up at the window of his parents' bedroom. It was wide open. He hesitated, closed the door and tiptoed down the garden path, still clutching his shoes. He kept looking back at the glaring eye of the open window, waiting for his father to lean out and shout after him.

At the bottom of the garden he put his shoes on, climbed over the fence and ran through the allotments to the fields on the hilltop. He was safe. It was as easy as winking. He smiled up at the moon. Why, it was as light as day. There was nothing to be afraid of: no one, nothing lying in wait to jump out on him. He could see for miles; surely? Those dark patches over there . . . were only bushes. Of course they were. Those long black octopus-arms groping along the ground towards him . . . were only the shadows of treetops moving in the wind. Of course they were. There was nothing to be scared of.

It became darker, clouds straggling across the moon. He began to whistle, looking everywhere; then held his breath to listen to the silence.

He stopped dead. Something was moving ahead. Something; someone: a faint rustling; louder, coming towards him.

From *Billy the Kid* by E. G. Thorpe

Comprehension

A 1. How old do you think Billy was?
2. Where did he feel safer?
3. Where was the top bolt?
4. Outside, was there pitch darkness, sunlight or moonlight?
5. What did he look at, before closing the door?
6. Why did he tiptoe down the path?
7. (a) Where did he stop to put on his shoes? (b) Why did he not put them on before?
8. (a) What were the dark patches? (b) Can you guess what he thought they were?
9. (a) What looked like the waving arms of an octopus? (b) What is an octopus?
10. What is the meaning of: hesitated, tiptoed, clutching, glaring, hilltop, straggling, a faint rustling?

B 1. Why do you think he held the key "with both hands to steady its turn"?
2. What time (o'clock) do you think it was? There are clues in the extract.
3. What time of year was it and what in the second paragraph tells us?
4. Why should the open window seem like a "glaring eye" to the boy?
5. (a) Why did he feel so *safe* when he reached the fields? (b) What had worried him?
6. What then began to worry him?
7. "He began to whistle, looking everywhere; then held his breath to listen . . ." What does this tell us about the boy? Choose one of these answers:
   He was musical. He was whistling his lost dog. He was afraid of the dark. He was lost.
8. "He stopped dead." (a) What does this mean? (b) Why did he do it?
9. Where do you think the boy is going? Choose one of these answers:
   (i) looking for his father (ii) escaping from prison (iii) joining his friends who are sleeping-out that night in the woods (iv) playing truant from school.
10. What is the meaning of: as easy as winking, as light as day, nothing lying in wait, octopus-arms, to listen to the silence, straggling, allotments?

Language

1. What are these collections or groups:

   a —— of lions, a —— or —— of cattle, a —— of geese, a swarm of —— (several), a —— of keys, a —— of grass, a clutch of ——, a —— of wool?

2. PHRASES, SENTENCES and PARAGRAPHS

   A *phrase* is not finished: it is part of a sentence.

   A *sentence* is complete and finished. It makes complete sense.

   A *paragraph* is usually several sentences. The sections of a story are paragraphs.

   Phrases: as black as jet   frightened mice   over and over again

   Sentences: The cat chased a mouse.   I shall come home early.

   Paragraphs: There are five paragraphs in the extract "Out at Night", so we should find five different sections or parts of the story:

   Paragraph 1: The boy creeps silently down the stairs and goes out of the house.
   Paragraph 2: He goes down the garden path, still worrying about being called back.
   Paragraph 3: He goes up the hill to the fields where he tries not to feel afraid.
   Paragraph 4: He becomes scared.
   Paragraph 5: He hears something coming towards him in the darkness.

   Say very briefly what would go into your paragraphs if you wrote a story about a boy who went out to the woods one night.

3. *Find the Stranger:* stairs   chairs   bedroom   fence   window

4. Fill in the missing verbs:

Present Tense	*Simple Past Tense*	*Past Tense with have, etc.*
You come too	You	You have . . . .
They	They took him . . .	They have . . . .
He	He	He has gone down
He	He told them	He has . . . .

5. Use one of these "sound-words" in a sentence: shout, whistle, rustling.

6. *Spelling* rooms: ki . . . . n   parl . . .   ba . . room

   I s . . pose you think you have done eno . . .   work today?

   Wel . . . .   your party g . ests politely.

7. ". . . nothing *lying* in wait to jump out on him . . ."

   Use *lying* and *laying* in two sentences.

8. What are these: Billy the *Kid*, a kid, cub, foal, calf, an eaglet?

9. The three on the left ALL HAVE *one* of the things in the brackets. Which one?

chairs, people, houses : (cushions, backs, decorations)
windows, clocks, telescopes : (rubber, glass, keys)
gardens, fields, forests : (fences, soil, walls, paths)
miles, rulers, races : (width, length, runners)
hills, skyscrapers, towers : (stones, glass, height, trees)

10. (a) Give the plural of: key, donkey, monkey, lady, penny, cherry.
(b) Give the singular of: shoes, patches, bushes, shelves, cargoes.

11. Put into alphabetical order: safe, stairs, steady, stand, shoe, shout.

12. Put in the apostrophe:
his parents bedroom, Billys shoes, one trees branches, a foxs yelp, cows tails, peoples stares, a towns parks, foxes brushes (tails).

13. Change to Indirect or Reported Speech:
"I tried hard not to be afraid of the dark," Billy said to his friends.

14. What does this word mean: abbreviation? Give an example.

15. Use in interesting sentences: the bottom of the stairs glaring eye long black octopus-arms shadows of treetops.

Find Out

1. Find out what these words mean, then use one from each group in sentences:
window, windmill, windfall (2), windscreen, windswept, windward
close (2), clothes, cloths patches, patchwork, pasture, pasteurised (why?)
staring, starling, starting (2), starving, stating, skating.

2. Find out the meaning of: open-handed, an open secret, open fire, open-eyed; stop dead, dead against an idea, dead asleep, dead beat, dead calm, as dead as a doornail, a dead faint, a dead heat, dead level, at dead of night, a dead secret, a dead shot, dead silence, dead slow, dead tired, a dead weight, dead of winter, dead on time, deadly.

3. Think of words which sound the same (or nearly the same) but which are spelt differently: stairs, key, eye, father, shoes.
Give the meaning of your words.

4. OUT AT NIGHT
Make a list of animals and birds which come out at night.
What do these words mean: nocturnal, vixen, holt, Brock, pipistrelle, owlet?

18

A Deafening Din

A noise like the roar of ten thousand angry lions came up from the pit. Beneath that noise there was another like the rumble of freight trains over a bridge. Then there was a higher note, the sound of escaping steam, like the hiss of a great serpent. And there were sudden explosions as if charges of dynamite were being set off.

The din became so terrific that when Dr. Dan spoke again no one could hear him.

Hal remembered what he had read in *Terry's Guide*: "Mt. Asama is the largest, angriest and most treacherous volcano in Japan. The dangers at the summit are manifold and should not be regarded lightly."

It was terrifying—and yet pleasant, because the heat rising from the fires beneath felt very good after a night in the chill fog. Each one of the visitors revolved like a chicken on a spit in order to warm himself all over.

From a bag that Hal carried, Dr. Dan produced various instruments, a thermometer, a pyroscope, a small spectroscope. He began to take readings and jot down the results in his notebook. He captured some of the rising gas in a test tube and put it away for later study.

He spoke again, but although the boys could see his lips move they could not hear a word. Dr. Dan signalled to the boys to follow him and set off along the edge of the crater.

From *Volcano Adventure* by Willard Price

Comprehension

A 1. The people are (visiting a zoo, standing on a volcano, at a coal-mine, waiting for a train at a station). Which?
2. Name any of these people.
3. Did they hear (a) trains rumbling over a bridge? (b) lions roaring in a pit?
4. If freight trains are not passenger trains, what are they?
5. Why could nobody hear Dr. Dan when he spoke?
6. What were the fires?
7. Why did everyone keep turning round?
8. What kind of signal do you think Dr. Dan made to the boys?
9. Where did Dr. Dan go?
10. What is the meaning of: angry lions, hiss, serpent, summit, terrifying, pleasant, escaping steam, various, chill fog, a chicken?

B 1. Where did all the noise come from? Do not answer: "from a pit".
2. Why are these mentioned: a serpent, a chicken, lions, trains, dynamite?
3. (a) Who caught some gas? (b) Why do you think he did this?
4. (a) What sort of notes do you think Dr. Dan made? (b) Why do you think he made them?
5. What special book do you think *Terry's Guide* may be?
6. Complete this: They were standing (at the top of, at the bottom of, halfway up) a —— called —— in the country of ——.
7. Why was it both frightening and pleasant to be there?
8. What had the previous night been like?
9. Can you think of *one* "reading" Dr. Dan would obtain from his instruments?
10. What is the meaning of: explosions, charges of dynamite, terrific, treacherous, manifold, revolved, a chicken on a spit, instruments, thermometer, volcano, should not be regarded lightly, jot down, the edge of the crater?

Language

1. Say whether these are phrases or sentences:
   (i) An angry dog (ii) An angry dog was barking. (iii) over the garden wall (iv) The batsman hit his wicket.

2\. ABBREVIATIONS

"*Dr*. Dan . . . *Mt*. Asama . . ." (See Key to Book Three, page 52.)

Dr. and Mt. are abbreviations or short ways of writing Doctor and Mount.

Abbreviations may be formed:

(i) by using initials (the first letters): J. S. Smith, B.B.C., P.T.O.

(ii) by missing out the middle or the ending of a word and putting a full stop to show that the word has been shortened: Dr., Capt.

(iii) by missing out letters and putting an apostrophe *in their place*: I'm, o'er

Say what these abbreviations mean:

B.B.C., P.T.O., Dr., Mt., Capt., o'er, I'm, can't, B.A., B.Sc., G.P.O., H.M.S., M.P., A.A., R.A.C., J.P., P.S., a.m., p.m., R.A.F.

Remember: Do *not* use apostrophe-abbreviations in Indirect or Reported Speech:

The man couldn't reach the top of the mountain. *Wrong*

The man could not reach the top of the mountain. *Right*

3\. *Find the Stranger:* roar rumble heat hiss

4\. Use these joining-words in sentences:

either . . . or, although, while, since.

5\. Think of words which mean the same as these words:

angry, beneath, serpent, sudden, din, largest, dangers, revolved.

6\. ". . . the heat *rising* from the fires . . . He captured some of the *rising* gas . . ."

Remember: We *raise* something, like a hat, the lid of a box or a flag.

We *rise* when we stand up.

Use *rise* and *raise* in sentences.

7\. Spell these words:

lives next door: n . . . . bour

looks after patients in hospital: n . . . .

naughty: mis . . . . . ous

assorted, mixed: var . . . s

ended well: suc . . . . ful

enough: suf . . . . ent

doing as one is told: ob . . . . nt

stubborn: ob . . . . . te

8\. Write correctly:

(i) vesuvius in italy is a very famous volcano which i have visited said hal

(ii) in exercise 18 we read a passage from volcano adventure by willard price

9\. Change to Direct Speech:

Dr. Dan told the boys to follow him along the edge of the crater but they did not hear him owing to the deafening noise all round them.

10. Pick a word out of the brackets to fit the space:

father, mother	:	brother, —— (nephew, sister, grandmother, aunt)
little, small	:	big, —— (elephant, large, tiny, mouse)
ice, cold	:	——, hot (skating, snow, fire, smoke)
windows, glass	:	doors, —— (frames, wood, walls, keys)
lessons, school	:	games, —— (bell, playground, teacher, football)

11. Put in the missing words:

	Comparing Two	*Comparing More*
high	higher	highest
noisy	——	——
——	——	angriest
——	——	largest
dim	——	——

12. Form nouns from these words, like this: happy, *happiness* (The happiness of . . .): various, pleasant, terrifying, warm, angriest, captured.
Use three of the nouns in sentences.

13. Give the plural of: volcano, gas, crater, edge, toe, tomato, piano.

14. Use in sentences: who's, whose.

15. Use in interesting sentences: angry lions rumble the largest terrifying.

Find Out

1. Find out what these words mean, then use one from each group in sentences:
rumble, rumple, ramble (2), ramshackle, ransack, ransom
terrific, terrifying, terrible
red, read (2), realise, recognises
signal, signature, signet, cygnet
crater, crate.

2. Find out the meaning of:
to be between two fires, playing with fire, to go through fire and water, Fire is a good servant but a bad master. A burnt child fears the fire.

3. Think of words which sound the same (or nearly the same) but which are spelt differently: higher, hear, read, there, a noise, great, boys.
Give the meaning of your words.

4. VOLCANOES
Find out all you can about volcanoes, especially Vesuvius which is more famous than Mt. Asama. Where is Vesuvius?
Find out about its famous eruption in Roman times, 1900 years ago.

19 *The Highwayman*

The wind was a torrent of darkness among the gusty trees,
The moon was a ghostly galleon tossed upon cloudy seas,
The road was a ribbon of moonlight over the purple moor,
And the highwayman came riding—
Riding—riding—
The highwayman came riding, up to the old inn-door.

He'd a French cocked-hat on his forehead, a bunch of lace at his chin,
A coat of claret velvet, and breeches of brown doeskin;
They fitted with never a wrinkle, his boots were up to the thigh!
And he rode with a jewelled twinkle,
His pistol butts a-twinkle,
His rapier hilt a-twinkle, under the jewelled sky.

Over the cobbles he clattered and clashed in the dark inn-yard,
And he tapped with his whip on the shutters, but all was locked and barred;
He whistled a tune to the window, and who should be waiting there
But the landlord's black-eyed daughter,
Bess, the landlord's daughter,
Plaiting a dark red love-knot into her long black hair.

From *The Highwayman* by Alfred Noyes

Comprehension

A 1. What was among the windswept trees?

2. (a) Did this happen during the day or night? (b) How do you know?
3. Where did the highwayman go?
4. How was he dressed: very elegantly, carelessly, untidily?
5. How long were his boots: to his thighs, knees, calves or ankles?
6. (a) Did he come silently and cautiously? (b) How do you know?
7. Who was waiting for him?
8. What was (a) white (b) brown (c) black (d) purple?
9. How do we know that this happened a long time ago? See how many different things in the extract tell you.
10. What is the meaning of: a bunch of lace, pistol butts, clattered and crashed, tapped with his whip, all was locked and barred, a highwayman?

B 1. How could the wind be a torrent and the moon a ghostly galleon (ship)?

2. Why was the moor purple?
3. (a) What kind of hat did he wear? (b) What do you think it was like?
4. The highwayman wore something red. Can you work out which word tells us?
5. Why did he ride with a "jewelled twinkle"?
6. How do we know that *the moon was shining* in a *starry* sky?
7. (a) Who loved the highwayman? (b) How do we know? (two answers).
8. How can we tell that the inn was in a lonely spot?
9. (a) Find five actions of the highwayman. (b) Find two actions of Bess. (c) What do you think the landlord was probably doing?
10. What is the meaning of: gusty trees, cloudy seas, The road was a ribbon of moonlight, velvet, rapier hilt, cobbles, shutters, whistled a tune to the window, plaiting a dark red love-knot?

Language

1. What do these abbreviations mean: can't, B.A., A.D., B.C., didn't, B.R., C.O.D. (explain), do., e.g., etc., R.N., Ave., St. (2)?
2. Put into their proper order, the shortest first: word, sentence, paragraph, phrase.

3. PRONOUNS

Here are some pronouns: I, me, my, myself, you, he, who, which.

PRONOUN means "in place of a noun". We use them so that we do not keep repeating the same noun.

Remember: (1) *Who* for people: I know a man *who* has six dogs.
Which for animals, birds, things: This is the pen *which* I lost.
(2) *Its* is a pronoun: The cat has hurt *its* tail.
It's means *it is*: "It's time for tea," said Mother.
(3) Jane and *I* went to the park. (Jane went, *I* went)
Let Jane and me go, please. (Let Jane go, let *me* go)
Give it to Fred and *me*. (to Fred, to *me*)

Write these sentences correctly:

(i) (Me and Bess, Bess and me, Bess and I) are friends.
(ii) (It's, Its) wheel is broken.
(iii) Fred is taller than (me, I).
(iv) The man (who, which, what) lives here told me to come.
(v) Between you and (me, I), I think (it's, its) unsafe.

4. ". . . clattered and clashed . . . tapped . . . whistled . . ."

These are verbs of SOUND.

(a) What verbs do we use for these animal-voices: an injured dog, a hungry wolf, a happy cat, an angry bull, a friendly horse, a frightened lamb?
(b) What verbs do we use for these noises: dry, dead leaves blown along the ground; church bells, a tiny bell, a stone falling down rocks, a closing door (in a strong draught), a door swinging on rusty hinges, a brook, a torrent, a watch, a dripping tap, machinery, noisy car-brakes?

5. *Remember* the difference in meaning between *can* and *may*.

CAN means "Am I able to do it, am I strong enough, is it too difficult for me?"
MAY means "Will you let me?"

Explain the difference in meaning here:

(i) "Can I climb in through the window?" said the highwayman.
(ii) "May I climb in through the window?" said the highwayman.

6. *Spelling* relations: un . . .   a . . t   ne . . ew   n . . ce
flowers: daf . . . . .   cro . . .   t . . ip

The ac . . dent hap . . . ed very sud . . . ly, without warning.

7. ALL ARE WHAT? Say what they all are on each line:
Durham, Cumberland, Devon, Norfolk, Kent
Humber, Thames, Ouse, Trent, Exe, Derwent
Ben Nevis, Snowdon, Kinder Scout, Scafell
Berlin, London, Paris, Brussels, Moscow

8. "... a *French* cocked-hat"
Give the adjectives formed from the nouns England, Holland, Canada, Wales, Ireland, Scotland, Switzerland, Spain, Norway and Denmark.

9. (a) Which words in the poem rhyme with trees, door, barred, hair?
(b) Which of these words rhymes with *friend*: fiend, reign, lend, field, ended?

10. "He'd a French cocked-hat on his forehead . . . the landlord's daughter . . ."
Say what the two apostrophes tell us.

11. Use the feminine of *landlord* and the masculine of *daughter* in a sentence.

12. *Find the Stranger:* clattered clashed tapped tossed whistled

13. (a) What are these: coastguards, poachers, tinkers, gamekeepers, wardens?
(b) What are these: a confectionery shop, a stationery shop, a Town Hall, an aquarium, a garage, museum, vineyard, granary, laundry, reservoir?

14. Use *twinkle* in two sentences: (i) as a noun (ii) as a verb.

15. Use in interesting sentences: the gusty trees a ghostly galleon
a ribbon of moonlight the old inn-door.

Find Out

1. Find out what these words mean, then use one from each group in sentences:
torrent, tortoise, torture, tornado, torpedo ghostly, ghastly
galleon, gallon, galley, gallery, gallows, gallop, gallant, gala
purple, purpose, pursue, purse (2) gusty, dusty, musty, rusty, trusty.

2. Find out the meaning of: sound in wind and limb, as swift as the wind, long-winded, the North Wind, a whirlwind; before long, long-standing, long-suffering, a long face, long division.

3. Think of words which sound the same (or nearly the same) but which are spelt differently: seas, inn, He'd, knot, hair, moor, to.
Give the meaning of your words.

4. OWN CHOICE
Choose a topic suggested by the three verses of "The Highwayman", like weather, water, ships, highwaymen, colours, etc., then find out all you can about it.

20

Trying to Remember

Stephen woke slowly from a confused dream. When he opened his eyes he saw roof beams above him, hung with dusty cobwebs. A spider dangled by a thread and wriggled its eight lively legs.

Still only half awake, Stephen watched the spider until it scuttled up the thread and disappeared. Then Stephen's gaze wandered to the latticed window. Near the window stood an empty bed with the covers tucked in rather sketchily as though the occupant had risen in a great hurry.

Of course, that's Harry's bed, thought Stephen, and here I am in Master Thomas's attic. But how did I get here?

Bit by bit, Stephen pieced together his vague memories. Philip had stabbed Gilbert at the Boar's Head, and there was a hue and cry. Philip had thrown Stephen off the roof of a house, and after that Stephen dimly remembered being carried along the street in the midst of many people.

But all these things had happened at sunset, and now it was broad daylight. Through the window Stephen heard the street noises—the clip-clop of a horse and the rumble of a wagon, women talking shrilly, and a pedlar calling, "What d'ye lack, ladies? What d'ye lack?"

As he listened, Stephen tenderly examined his cuts and bruises.

From *Three Golden Nobles* by Christine Price

Three Golden Nobles is a story about life in England around 1356.

Comprehension

A 1. What had Stephen just been doing?
2. What did he see first of all?
3. (a) What was the spider doing? (b) Where did it go?
4. (a) What in that room belonged to Harry? (b) Describe it.
5. What did Stephen ask himself?
6. What did he remember rather hazily or vaguely?
7. What had happened to him after he was thrown off a roof?
8. What street noises could he hear?
9. What did he do while listening to the noises outside?
10. What is the meaning of: roof beams, dusty cobwebs, scuttled up the thread, disappeared, sunset, broad daylight, clip-clop?

B 1. What kind of dream is a "confused" one?
2. Why did Stephen think that someone had been in a great hurry?
3. (a) In whose house was Stephen? (b) In which part of the house?
4. (a) Do you think he had been there before? (b) How do you know?
5. Why did he remember vaguely, not clearly?
6. (a) Who had been stabbed? (b) When? (c) Where had it happened?
7. What would the "Boar's Head" be?
8. Why do you think Stephen had been thrown off the roof of a house?
9. Find all the clues which suggest that this is a story about olden times.
10. Give the meaning of: Stephen's gaze wandered, eight lively legs, latticed window, rather sketchily, occupant, Bit by bit, pieced together, a hue and cry, dimly remembered, talking shrilly, pedlar, "What d'ye lack?"

Language

1. Write correctly:
   (i) Jane is smaller than (I, me).
   (ii) The mouse bolted back into (its, it's) hole in the corner.
   (iii) Janet, Joan and (I, me) went carol-singing.
   (iv) "(Can, May) I go out, please?" asked John politely.

2. PREPOSITIONS

Words like under, at, by, for, from, in, of, off, to, up, with, etc. are called PREPOSITIONS, because they are *pre-positioned* (placed in front of other words) to complete the meaning.

Meaning not complete: The old lady is fond —— cats.
The apples were —— the basket —— the shelf.

Meaning complete: The old lady is fond *of* cats.
The apples were *in* the basket *on* the shelf.

Remember: fell *off* the tree   fell out *of* the car
different *from* something else
agree *with* someone, be angry *with* someone, meddle *with* something
be ashamed *of*, tired *of* something, full *of* (but filled *with*)

Put in the missing words:

(i) The mischievous boy must apologise —— his bad behaviour.
(ii) The cat jumped out —— the window.
(iii) The ball —— wool fell —— the table.
(iv) —— the eaves swallows are nesting.
(v) I am tired —— your laziness. You ought to be ashamed —— yourself.
(vi) John's new overcoat is different —— mine.

3. Use in sentences: laid, lain.

4. What do these words mean: *pieced* together; pierced?
Use *pierced* in a sentence.

5. What do the apostrophes tell us in this: ". . . that's Harry's bed . . ."?

6. (a) Give the plural of spider, thread, attic, cry, roof, hoof, boar's head.
(b) Write this, changing all the singulars to plurals:
He watched the spider until it scuttled up the thread and disappeared.

7. *Find the Stranger:* Stephen Philip Gilbert Christine Harry

8. Make the second pair agree in the same way that the first pair agree:

London, England	:	Edinburgh, ——
dog, kennel	:	tame rabbit, ——
spring, summer	:	——, winter
beech, tree	:	armchair, ——
lion, roars	:	——, brays
typist, office	:	mechanic, ——
flock, sheep	:	——, whales

9. Think of words which mean the same, or nearly the same, as these words: disappeared, above, wriggled, remembered, hurry, vague.
10. Think of words which are the opposites of slowly, opened, above, empty (bed), dimly, remembered, daylight, shrilly.
11. What are *all* the meanings of hue, bit, cry?
12. Put into alphabetical order: eyes, eight, empty, eyesight, eighth.
13. The following pairs are mixed up. Sort them out like this: web, spider.
    sleep, kitchen   *web*, dream   boy, *spider*   cook, Stephen   night, wound
    robin, animal   cart, day   wolf, horse   bandages, bird
14. *Spelling*   insects: . nat   mos . . . to   bu . . . . fly
    fruit: ban . . .   cur . . . . s   ras . . . . s
    There were hund . . . s   of col . . . ed   li . . ts   decorating the seafront.
    Did you have a   ple . . . nt   jo . . ney   from London?
15. Use in interesting sentences: a confused dream   dusty cobwebs
    vague memories   hue and cry   talking shrilly.

Find Out

1. Find out what these words mean, then use one from each group in sentences: wriggled, waggled, waddled, wrinkled, writhed, wrestled, wretched, wrecked
   slowly, slyly, sluggishly, slovenly (adjective)   scuttle (3), scuffle, scurry, scullery, scullion   appear, disappear, reappear   assemble, reassemble, resemble.
2. Find out the meaning of: plans all cut and dried, to cut and run, cut someone short when speaking, cut someone dead, a short cut, cut down, a cut-purse, a cut-throat, cut up rough, very cut up.
3. Think of words which sound the same (or nearly the same) but which are spelt differently: boar's, thrown, eye, saw, eight, great.
   Give the meaning of your words.
4. THE MIDDLE AGES
   When were the Middle Ages? What were guilds or gilds, trade-signs, apprentices, bull-baiting, water-carriers, the stocks, pillory, cut-purses, vagabonds?

21 *Salmo*

In his second year Salmo became a parr, with roundish brown marks rather like finger-prints on his sides, and looked like a trout, only a little more shapely and graceful. He was still content with the river, though he moved from pool to pool more often as time went on. Then, early in his third year, when he was about six inches long, he changed a good deal in appearance, becoming a silver smolt, and for the first time felt the mysterious tug of the sea. It made him restless; and, without knowing where he was going or why, he set off on the first of his long journeys.

Down the river he went, along with other smolts like himself, till he came to the estuary and was aware of a difference in the water, a tang that was strangely exciting. He jerked his strong tail and swam faster, eager to enter the sea. The river current mingled with the incoming tide, fresh water with salt, and cross-currents came sweeping up the coast; but Salmo swam right ahead towards the ocean that somehow seemed to be the right place for him to live in now.

Enemies were waiting for the smolts: big codfish that snapped at them as they swam out beyond the tidal bar, and hungry gulls and cormorants, diving from the surface of the sea. But Salmo passed them and swam on and on; and soon he was hunting, too, snapping at fishes smaller than himself.

The sea was even richer in food than the river had been. All the year round Salmo could catch as much as he needed; and he grew big and strong and became a grilse. Some of the smolts which had journeyed with him returned to the river at this grilse stage, when they were about three and a half years old; but Salmo stayed on in the sea for some time longer, feeding and growing and becoming a splendid salmon.

From *Round the Year Stories* by Maribel Edwin

Comprehension

A 1. This passage is about a (dog, fish, boy, fruit, river). Which?
2. What did Salmo become first of all?
3. (a) What is a trout? (b) Is a trout more graceful than Salmo?
4. (a) How long is a smolt? (b) What colour is it?
5. What did Salmo do when he became restless?
6. (a) Why did he go down the river? (b) Did he go alone?
7. Why was there "fresh water with salt"?
8. Which three enemies were waiting for Salmo and his friends?
9. Which had more food: the sea or the river?
10. What is the meaning of: finger-prints, roundish brown marks rather like finger-prints, shapely and graceful, from pool to pool, long journeys, jerked his strong tail, the river current?

B 1. This is a story about a —— named ——.
2. What is an estuary? How can you tell from clues in the second paragraph?
3. What is "the mysterious tug of the sea"?
4. Why did the water in the estuary have a strangely exciting tang?
5. What were the smolts' enemies: animals, birds, fish or men?
6. Salmo grew from a —— to a —— to a —— to a ——.
7. (a) Which fish returned to the river: parrs, smolts or grilses?
(b) How old were they?
8. Are salmon freshwater fish, salt-water fish or both?
9. What are (a) brown (b) silver (c) restless (d) strong (e) big (f) hungry?
10. What is the meaning of: still content with the river, changed in appearance, the incoming tide, cross-currents, the tidal bar, cormorants, codfish, gulls, at this grilse stage?

Language

1. Put suitable prepositions (like *of*, *in*, *from*, etc.) into the spaces:
   (i) —— the accident, the boy complained —— a pain —— his right leg.
   (ii) The boy fell out —— the tree, then fell —— a swing.

2. MORE ABOUT COMPARING THINGS

   In Exercise 9 we talked about comparing things: good, better, best.

   We saw that adjectives usually add ER and EST.

   Long adjectives do *not* do this, as it would make them far too long and difficult to say. Instead, they borrow *more* and *most*: more beautiful, most beautiful: This painting is *beautiful* but this here is *more beautiful*, while the one over there is the *most beautiful* one of all.

   Do the same with these long adjectives: splendid, graceful, mysterious.

   Most adverbs are *long* words too, so they do the same:
   carefully, more carefully, most carefully.

   Do the same with these long adverbs: generously, greedily, angrily.

   Use the correct form of the word in the brackets:
   (i) (obstinate): He is the . . . . boy I have ever met.
   (ii) (careless): You are . . . . than Roger.
   (iii) (carelessly): Your work today has been done . . . . than ever before.

3. Here is a list of parents, father first, then mother. What do we call their young ones: gander and goose, dog-fox and vixen, stallion and mare, drake and duck, tiger and tigress, lion and lioness?

4. *Spelling* animals: ba . . er buf . . . o ele . . . . t gir . . . . gor . . . .
   We had a very ex . . ting a . vent . . . yesterday.
   Weasels are f . . rce, dan . . . ous ani . . . s which hunt rabbits.

5. Use one word out of each set of brackets:
   (i) My (nephew, niece) has (wrote, written) to me about her kitten.
   (ii) We can (beat, win) (there, their) netball team if we play really (good, well).
   (iii) What strange (weather, whether) we are having lately!
   (iv) The salmon (swum, swam) faster, feeling (quite, quiet) excited.
   (v) The small boy (rang, rung) our doorbell and (run, ran) away.

6. *Find the Stranger:* swallow sparrow salmon seagull starling

7. Write correctly:
   i feel restless said salmo the salmon i must go down to the sea

8. Give (a) the plural of trout, salmon, estuary
(b) the singular of journeys, fishes, chimneys, finches, enemies.

9. *Salmo* the Salmon
What special or pet names do we give to these creatures, like Leo the Lion: the fox (R——), bear (B——), badger (B——), parrot (P——), robin (R——)?

10. Complete these similes: as —— as a fox, as —— as a kitten, as —— as a peacock, as —— as a bee, as —— as a lamb, as —— as an eel.

11. Use these two joining-words in sentences: unless, before.

12. What are *all* the meanings of second, tug, sweep, right, catch?

13. Use two of these "sound-words" in sentences: gurgle, snarl, twitter, crash.

14. Add adverbs and suitable endings:
(i) The road-makers worked . . . .
(ii) I was waiting . . . .
(iii) The hungry fox crept . . . .

15. Use in interesting sentences: finger-prints shapely and graceful the mysterious tug strangely exciting hungry.

Find Out

1. Find out what these words mean, then use one from each group in sentences:
parr, parry, parrot, parson, parsnip, parsley, parlour, particle, particular (2), partition, partner, partridge stage (2), stag, stagger, stagnant content, contents, contented, discontented made, maid right (2), write.

2. Find out the meaning of: like water off a duck's back, in hot water, spend money like water, as weak as water, throw cold water on a plan; made it up (2), make off with it, make-believe, make do, make and mend, make light of something, make room, Make hay while the sun shines.

3. Think of words which sound the same (or nearly the same) but which are spelt differently: tide, tail, side, more, time, current.
Give the meaning of your words.

4. YOUNG ONES
Make a list of young animals and birds.
What is the difference between a foal, a colt and a filly; a chick and a chicken?
What are born in eyries, earths, setts, lodges, forms and dreys?

Night Mail

This is the night mail crossing the border,
Bringing the cheque and the postal order,
Letters for the rich, letters for the poor,
The shop at the corner and the girl next door.
Pulling up Beattock, a steady climb—
The gradient's against her, but she's on time.

Past cotton grass and moorland boulder
Shovelling white steam over her shoulder,
Snorting noisily as she passes
Silent miles of wind-bent grasses.

Birds turn their heads as she approaches,
Stare from the bushes at her black-faced coaches
Sheep dogs cannot turn her course,
They slumber on with paws across.
In the farm she passes no one wakes,
But a jug in the bedroom gently shakes.

Dawn freshens, the climb is done.
Down towards Glasgow she descends . . .

From *Night Mail* by W. H. Auden

Comprehension

A 1. The poem "Night Mail" is about (a knight in armour, a postman, a train, a steamer). Which?

2. Who receive letters?
3. What does the night mail pass very noisily?
4. What are "wind-bent grasses"?
5. Who is "she" in line 11?
6. (a) Who sleeps? (b) What sleeps?
7. (a) Why does a jug shake? (b) Where is it, exactly?
8. (a) Does the land slope upwards or downwards into Glasgow? (b) Which word tells us?
9. Can you guess where the night mail may have come from?
10. What is the meaning of: she's on time, boulder, snorting, approaches, with paws across, gently shakes?

B 1. You can hear a rhythm or steady beat if you say this poem. What does it sound like?

2. How do we know that part of the route is very lonely?
3. Which border does the night mail cross? From —— to ——.
4. (a) What must Beattock be? (b) The gradient is (a red signal, a green signal, a slope, a station, a signalman). Which?
5. Why is "shovelling" a vivid, descriptive word in line 8?
6. Explain "her *black-faced* coaches". (Think what kind of train it is.)
7. Try to explain line 13.
8. At what time of day or night do you think the night mail arrives in Glasgow?
9. Line 4 means that the night mail brings letters for (the shop at the corner near the poet's house and the girl who lives next door to him; the shop near your house and the girl next door to you; many shops and many people). Which?
10. What is the meaning of: cheque, postal order, a steady climb, The gradient's against her, slumber on, Dawn freshens, she descends, cotton grass?

Language

1. Put in the missing words:

	Comparing two	*Comparing more*
big	bigger	biggest
dreadful		
noisily		

2. LETTER-WRITING

Make sure that you can write letters properly and address envelopes properly:

100, High St.,
Danesby,
Yorkshire.
(Post code here)
(*Date here*)

Dear Roger,

Thank you for your kind invitation . . . .

Yours sincerely,
David

Remember: (1) Proper punctuation, abbreviations and position of all parts.

(2) In addressing the envelope, start halfway down, leaving room for the postmark, etc. stamped on it in the Post Office. Write the name of the TOWN in capital letters, to make sorting and delivery easier.

Draw an envelope and address it to a friend, then begin and end a letter.

3. ALL HAVE WHAT ? The first one is done to help you.

chairs, boys, girls, tables	*all have*	(wood, *legs*, heads, clothes)
eagles, sparrows, robins	:	(mountains, gardens, red breasts, wings)
houses, bungalows, cinemas	:	(managers, flats, doors, beds)
shower, rainstorm, cloudburst	:	(thunder, rain, sunshine, lightning)
trees, plants, grass	:	(acorns, roots, branches, lawns)

4. *Find the Stranger:* gradient climb slumber descent ascent slope
5. Use *bring* and *fetch* in sentences.
6. Think of *all* the meanings of letters, border, passes, order, course, pull up.
7. (a) Write a phrase. (b) Write a sentence. (c) What is a paragraph?
8. What is the meaning of: "The *gradient's* against her, but *she's* on time."? What do we call the "high comma"?
9. (a) Which words in the poem rhyme with climb, boulder, coaches, wakes? (b) Which of these words rhymes with *though*: cough, plough, blow, bough, threw?

10. Find in your dictionary the words beginning with *ex* which mean:
(i) completely tired out (ii) to put out a light or fire (iii) Way Out (iv) cry out (v) explains something (vi) a fast train (vii) bursting loudly (viii) costly
Use two of your answers in sentences.

11. Pick out the Proper nouns and write them properly (the whole phrase where necessary): glasgow, the night mail, "night mail", king, king charles I, down the street, london road, the road to london, a winding river, the river.

12. *Spelling* animals: l . . pard kang . . . . ze . . . squi . . . . r . . ndeer
The thun . . . and light . . . . were very fri . . . . . ing.

13. Change to Indirect or Reported Speech:
(i) "Why haven't you rung the bell?" the teacher asked the monitor.
(ii) "I missed the train," John said to his friend outside the station.

14. Give the Present tense or time of these verbs: began, blew, have broken, chose, clung, drew, drove, fought, has forgotten, froze, has woven, written.

15. Use in interesting sentences: the night mail the shop at the corner moorland snorting noisily silent miles.

Find Out

1. Find out what these words mean, then use one from each group in sentences:
postal, postcard, postmark, postage, poster, post (2), post-haste, P.S.
mail (2), male gradient, gradual, grade, radiant, radiator
shakes, stakes, steaks, stokes, stocks (2), stoker.

2. Find out the meaning of: pass away (2), come to pass, bring to pass, pass over something (2), a password; in a tight corner, a blind corner; The early bird catches the worm. Birds of a feather flock together. A bird in hand is worth two in the bush. Kill two birds with one stone.

3. Think of words which sound the same (or nearly the same) but which are spelt differently: mail, border, cheque, boulder, paws, knight, past.
Give the meaning of your words.

4. RAILWAYS
In your atlas follow the route of the Queen of Scots express from London to Glasgow: London, Peterborough, Grantham, Doncaster, Leeds, Harrogate, Darlington, Newcastle, Berwick-on-Tweed, Edinburgh, Falkirk, Glasgow.
In which counties are these towns or cities?

23 *Old London Bridge*

In front of her the river shimmered in the sunlight of a bright spring morning. It looked like a big lake shut in on three sides by banks of houses. On the north side the buildings all around her crowded down to the water's edge, ending in a broken line of wharfs and warehouses and a jumble of roofs. Opposite, on the south bank, there were gardens among the houses and a background of tree-tops to mark the open country.

Between the north bank and the south, like a great wall across the river, lay London Bridge which had a street of houses and shops all the way along it, and, into the bargain, a gatehouse and a drawbridge and even a chapel with pinnacles and turrets, all built upon its massive arches and buttresses.

The tide was at the flood and the water lay high against the Bridge, so calm that a second Bankside and a second Bridge were reflected upside down upon its surface. But soon the tide would turn and then the river would rush back seawards through the narrow arches, roaring and groaning like an imprisoned beast, sucking into rapids and whirlpools anything that came in its way.

Nan knew the sound of it well, for their old nurse, Goody Doubleday, lived on the Bridge, and sometimes, for a great treat, she was allowed to stay the night with Goody. She loved to lie cosily in bed listening to the noises that the water made as it gushed underneath the house.

But at this moment everything seemed very quiet. The little ships tied up by the wharfs all lay in idleness, their brightly coloured sails furled. No work was being done, no cargoes loaded or unloaded, for it was Ascension Day, a holy-day, and the few people to be seen were either fishing from the quays or lounging about and gossiping.

From *Ring out Bow Bells* by Cynthia Harnett

Ring Out Bow Bells is a story about life in England in 1415.

Comprehension

A 1. What was the name of the girl who was looking at the river?
2. At what time of the year did this take place?
3. What was the weather like?
4. On how many sides of the river were there houses?
5. What was like a wall across the river?
6. (a) Was it high or low tide? (b) How do you know?
7. (a) What was like a caged beast? (b) When?
8. (a) Were the gardens on the same side of the river as the girl? (b) What tells us?
9. How was the old London Bridge different from modern bridges?
10. What is the meaning of: shimmered, buildings, a jumble of roofs, wharfs, gatehouse, drawbridge, chapel, reflected, surface, rapids and whirlpools, treat, cosily, cargoes?

B 1. Why did the river appear to be shut in on three sides?
2. (a) On which bank of the river was the girl?
(b) Which bank had fields and woods close by?
3. Which words in the second paragraph mean (a) spires (b) towers (c) supports?
4. Why were there two Banksides and two London Bridges?
5. (a) Where did Goody Doubleday live? (b) How could she?
6. Why was it very peaceful near the river on this particular morning?
7. (a) What were people doing? (b) What kind of work did the men usually do?
8. Why do you think London Bridge had narrow arches?
9. (a) What sparkled? (b) What were idle? (c) What were rolled up?
10. What is the meaning of: banks of houses, crowded down to the water's edge, a broken line of wharfs and warehouses, a background of tree-tops, open country, massive arches, at the flood, seawards, gushed, lay in idleness, a holy-day, lounging about and gossiping?

Language

1. How would you begin and end a letter to a friend?
Where should we start the address on an envelope? Why?

2. PREFIX

"No work was being done, no cargoes loaded or *unloaded* . . ."

We can make new words by adding to the beginning of words: load, *unload.*

We can often make *opposites* by adding to the front of words: *im*possible, *in*visible, *un*happy, *dis*contented.

(a) Make words of opposite meaning by adding to the front of these words: ripe, true, patient, perfect, complete, convenient, credible

(b) Add *im*, *sub* or *fore* to make new words: head marine polite

Remember: Letters added to the front of words are called a PREFIX.

3. (a) What do we call the homes of gipsies, royalty, monks, nuns, lions, cows?
   (b) Who or what live in barracks, a vicarage, an eyrie, a drey, kennel, sty?

4. *Find the Stranger:* lake tide wharf river rapids

5. Make six *double words*, like *sunlight* (sun, light), from these twelve words: table, board, cup, spoon, cloth, egg, man, house, black, tea, light, police.

6. Which is the correct word?
   (i) Nan was glad to (except, accept) the invitation.
   (ii) Everyone worked hard, (except, accept) on holy-days.

7. (a) Give the singular of: buttresses, warehouses, wharfs, cargoes, roofs.
   (b) Give the plural of: edge, arch, nurse, quay, hoof.

8. Fill in the gaps with prepositions (like *to, of, from,* etc.):
   —— olden times, London Bridge had a street —— houses and shops —— it. This was different —— the London Bridge —— today.

9. Place each adjective with a suitable noun from the list:
   adjectives: ruined, dangerous, piercing, interesting, stormy, anxious, sufficient, barren, valuable, obedient.
   nouns: corner, scream, child, castle, mother, sea, island, ring, story, food.

10. Put into alphabetical order: quiet, quite, queen, quick, queer, quickly.

11. *Spelling* birds: can . . . cuc . . . ni . . . . . gale pen . . . . pig . . .
    He is a very fam . . ., skil . . l artist.
    As the train ap . . . . ched the sta . . . n the pas . . . . ers became excited.

12. Make the second pair agree in the same way that the first pair agree:

April, spring	:	October, ——
river, flowed	:	bird, ——
cold, hot	:	happy, ——

herd, buffalo	:	——, herring
door, slams	:	whip, ——
bull, bellows	:	cow, ——
England, Englishman	:	Canada, ——
lord, lady	:	tiger, ——

13. BETWEEN and AMONG

Remember: between is about *two* things, *among* is about *more than two.*
We divide something *between* two people but *among* more than two people.
Use *between* and *among* in sentences.

14. Choose the correct words:
    (i) I have (forgot, forgotten) your name.
    (ii) The bird has (flew, flown, flowed) away.
    (iii) Why have you (taken, took) my book?
    (iv) (Write, Right) down a list of shops (were, where, wear) fireworks are sold.
    (v) I am sure you must (of, have) done it.

15. Use in interesting sentences: a bright spring morning   reflected
    a jumble of roofs   roaring and groaning   brightly coloured sails.

Find Out

1. Find out what these words mean, then use one from each group in sentences:
   shimmer, shiver, shrivel, shrink, shriek   a lounge, lounger, lunge
   stumble, grumble, jumble, mumble, tumble, fumble, crumble, humble, rumble
   treat, tread, treacle, treason, treachery, threat, thresh, threshold, three-fold.
2. Find out the meaning of: as sound as a bell, Empty vessels make the most sound. pass with flying colours, colourless, colourful, off colour, change colour, colour up, colour-blind; well-to-do, leave well alone, well-read, well-off, well-tried, well-worn, well-behaved, well known, Well done! All's well that ends well. Well begun is half done.
3. Think of words which sound the same (or nearly the same) but which are spelt differently: knew, way, tied, seen, its, quay, were, there, so.
   Give the meaning of your words.
4. LONDON
   Find out all you can about London: St. Paul's Cathedral, the Tower of London, Westminster Abbey, Big Ben, Cleopatra's Needle, Nelson's Column, Eros, the Serpentine, Beefeaters, P.L.A., etc.

24

The King of the Blue Seas

In the glorious town of Novgorod there once lived a minstrel named Sadko. He possessed but little gold, and to earn money he went round the noble feasts and banquets and enchanted everyone, princes, boyars, and merchants alike, with his marvellous skill on the gusly, the Russian psaltery. One day, however, misfortune befell him, for no one that day summoned him to play at any feast or banquet. Then a second and a third day passed, and still the minstrel Sadko remained without hire, and sighing deeply, he went down to the shores of Lake Ilmen, sat in the shade of a rock and began to pluck the strings of his maplewood gusly. He played thus all day, and just as evening was falling, the waves of the lake suddenly swirled and roared and the waters were clouded with sand. Sadko was terrified and running away from the lake he returned to the town of Novgorod.

The dark night passed and the light of day came again, but still no one invited Sadko to play at a feast, and finding his enforced idleness most tedious, the minstrel went again down to the shores of Lake Ilmen, sat in the shade of the burning rock, and began to play. He played all day, and as dusk fell, the waves of the lake suddenly swirled and roared and the waters were clouded with sand, and Sadko ran away and returned to Novgorod.

And still on the third day no one invited Sadko to a feast, and again he went down to the shores of Lake Ilmen and played all day in the shade of the burning rock. And as dusk fell on the third evening, the waves of the lake suddenly swirled and roared and the waters were clouded with sand. This time, however, Sadko was not afraid, and he continued to pluck the strings of the psaltery on the shore of the lake. And then, when he had played thus for some time, the waves of the lake suddenly swirled and roared louder than ever, and before the terrified minstrel could move a limb, the waters parted, and out of the lake stepped the mighty figure of the great King of the Blue Seas!

From *Russian Tales and Legends* by Charles Downing

Comprehension

A 1. What was the minstrel's name?
2. (a) Was he rich or poor? (b) How do you know?
3. What tree had been used to make his musical instrument?
4. Why was he unhappy?
5. On which day did he go down to the lake for the first time?
6. What did he do there?
7. What happened (a) on his first visit? (b) on his second visit?
8. What happened on his third visit?
9. Why did Sadko run away?
10. What is the meaning of: to earn money, noble feasts, sighing deeply, the shores of Lake Ilmen, sat in the shade of a rock, pluck the strings?

B 1. (a) In which country do you think Novgorod is? (b) Why do you think so?
2. If "boyars" come between princes and merchants in importance, what do you think "boyars" were?
3. (a) What was a gusly? (b) Describe how it was used. (c) What was a psaltery?
4. How did Sadko earn his living?
5. (a) Why did the lake water become cloudy? (b) What can make this happen to an ordinary lake or pond?
6. Was it freezing, cold, warm, hot or very hot by the lake?
7. Why do you think Sadko was afraid twice but not the third time?
8. Besides being told by the title of the book, how can we tell that this story is a legend?
9. What did Sadko find very annoying on the second day?
10. What is the meaning of: glorious town, possessed but little gold, banquets, enchanted everyone, his marvellous skill, misfortune befell him, summoned him, without hire, his en*forced* idleness, as dusk fell, he continued, the mighty figure, the King of the Blue Seas?

Language

1. Add prefixes to these words:
(a) to make opposites: happy, possible, correct, agree
(b) not to make opposites: the ..coming tide, Cross the road by the ...way underneath! Please ..turn your library book. Water will ..fresh you.

2. COMMON MISTAKES

(1) **Practice** and **Practise, etc.**

Sadko had *a long practice* every day. He had *to practise* every day.

Remember: The C spelling is the *noun*. The S spelling is the *verb*.

(i) c: *n*oun s: *v*erb c,n s,v in alphabetical order

or (ii) Think of *advice* and *advise* where you can *hear* the difference:

good advice (noun) I will advise you what to do. (verb)

Use in sentences: practice, practise, prophesy, licence.

The *verb* may be prophesy, prophesied, advised, licensed, practising, etc.

The *noun* may be singular or plural: many prophecies, a licence, football practices.

(2) **Current** and **Currant**

Remember: curr*e*nt: E for *e*lectricity. (An electric current flows along. So does a current of water. CURRANT is a fruit.)

(3) **Stationery** and **Stationary**

Remember: station*e*ry: E for *e*nvelopes, etc. Station*a*ry: standing still.

Use *current* and *stationary* in sentences.

3. Give the name of the people and the adjective, like Russia (*Russians, Russian*): Belgium, Denmark, Scotland, Portugal, Poland, Switzerland, France, Holland.
4. *Find the Stranger:* waves waters lake rock sea
5. Put into their proper order of time: evening, 2 p.m., midday, 9 a.m., dawn.
6. What is the difference in meaning between the two words in each pair: an isle and an aisle; a beach and a beech; a border and a boarder; a bow and a bough (same pronunciation); a boy and a buoy; a ceiling and sealing-wax; celery and salary; cereals and serials; a cellar and a seller?
7. Write these sentences correctly:
   (i) Sadko could not earn money (nowhere, anywhere).
   (ii) He could not do (nothing, anything) about it.
   (iii) The lazy boy did not know (nothing, anything) about the lesson.
8. Write correctly:
   sadko lived in novgorod a town in russia he was a minstrel who played at feasts and banquets one day nobody hired him whatever shall i do said sadko when this had happened several times
9. Pick out the adverb and use it in a sentence: Novgorod, lived, little, to, but, he, marvellous, suddenly, glorious.

10. Which verb fits each sentence: spoke, sighed, shouted, swirled?

(i) The minstrel —— in despair.

(ii) "Who is playing by my lake?" —— the King of the Blue Seas.

(iii) The lake —— and foamed angrily.

(iv) Sadko —— to the mighty king.

11. Change to Direct Speech:

(i) The porter said that the next train to London would leave from Platform 9.

(ii) The policeman ordered the crowd to stand back.

12. We find stories like the one about Sadko in a book of legends. What do we find in the following: an atlas, a telephone directory, an encyclopaedia, a diary, a calendar, a dictionary, a library, a museum, a catalogue, a reference book?

13. *Spelling* birds: spar . . . swal . . . star . . . . t . . ush . ren

Our impor . . . . visit . . s had come a long dis . . . . . by train.

14. Change these verbs from the Past to the Present tense or time:

he carried, she scrubbed, it splashed, has flown away, has broken.

15. Use in interesting sentences: earn money in the shade of a rock suddenly swirled marvellous burning.

Find Out

1. Find out what these words mean, then use one from each group in sentences:

limb, lamb, lame, lament   terrified, terrible   horrified, horrible

minstrel, minister (2)   seas, sees, seize, siege, besieged

possess, possible, postponed, postscript   marvellous, mysterious.

2. Find out the meaning of: to live and let live, a matter of life and death, a danger to life and limb, have the time of one's life, a lifeboat, lifebelt, to run for dear life, the livelong day, lifeless, lively, While there's life, there's hope!

3. Think of words which sound the same (or nearly the same) but which are spelt differently: hire, blue, time, him, passed, great.

Give the meaning of your words.

4. LEGENDS and FAIRY-TALES

Who were the following:

Hans Christian Andersen, the Brothers Grimm, Aesop, King Arthur, Robin Hood, William Tell, the Ugly Duckling, the Little Matchgirl, Hansel and Gretel, Snow White, Sleeping Beauty?

25

Summer Song

There are white moon daisies in the mist of the meadow
Where the flowered grass scatters its seeds like spray,
There are purple orchis by the wood-ways' shadow,
There are pale dog-roses by the white highway;
And the grass, the grass is tall, the grass is up for hay,
With daisies white like silver and the buttercups like gold,
And it's oh! for once to play thro' the long, the lovely day,
To laugh before the year grows old!

There is silver moonlight on the breast of the river
Where the willows tremble to the kiss of night,
Where the nine tall aspens in the meadow shiver,
Shiver in the night wind that turns them white.
And the lamps, the lamps are lit, the lamps the glow-worms light,
Between the silver aspens and the west's last gold.
And it's oh! to drink delight in the lovely lonely night,
To be young before the heart grows old!

E. Nesbit

Comprehension

A 1. What look like the moon?

2. In the meadow it is (sunny, raining, misty, dark). Which?
3. What is the grass doing?
4. Which flowers are (a) purple (b) white (c) golden (d) pale?
5. Which flowers grow near the road?
6. What is lonely?
7. The moonlight shines on the (sea, lake, mountains, river, lamps). Which?
8. (a) How many tall trees are in the meadow? (b) What kind are they?
9. Whose lamps are lit?
10. What is the meaning of: mist, meadow, flowered grass, purple, hay, tremble, the lovely lonely night?

B 1. Where are the daisies growing?

2. Explain the second line of the poem.
3. What does the poet think we should do in the summer daytime?
4. How can we "drink delight in the lovely lonely night"? It does not mean drink.
5. Verse 1 tells us about the ——. Verse 2 tells us about the ——. Put one word into each space.
6. The aspen is called the Trembling Poplar because its leaves (pale underneath) are always shivering. How does this explain line 4 in the second verse?
7. What in the second verse tells us that night has only just come?
8. (a) Name all the flowers in the poem. (b) Name all the trees in the poem.
9. (a) Which flower likes shady places? (b) Which tree likes damp places?
10. What is the meaning of: the grass is up for hay, before the year grows old, before the heart grows old, the kiss of night, the night wind?

Language

1. What is the difference in meaning between stationery and stationary; current and currant; practice and practise?
2. WORDS JOINED TOGETHER

   What do you notice about these words from the poem *Summer Song*: wood-ways, dog-roses, highway, buttercups, moonlight, glow-worms?

Make twelve new words by joining together a word from each section. (The word from Section A does not have to come first.):

A: black, mill, cup, tea, church, well, brush, cloth, apple, shed, lamp, grand

B: spoon, stand, board, yard, ink, egg, tooth, pine, water, coal, light, table

Remember: Words joined together are called COMPOUND WORDS.

3. BORROW and LEND

Remember: (i) You borrow something *from* someone: May I borrow it, please?
(ii) You lend something *to* someone: I will lend you my crayons.

Remember: Politeness ("*Please*") and "*May* I . . .?" NOT "Can I . . .?"

Use *borrow* and *lend* in sentences.

4. (a) Change all nouns, pronouns and verbs to the plural:
(i) There is a strange purple flower in the field.
(ii) The reindeer has hurt its foot.

(b) Change to the singular:
(i) There are nine tall aspens near the willows.
(ii) The ladies were helping to make the Fairies' costumes for the School Concert.

5. *Find the Stranger:* daisies orchids orchards dog-roses

6. (a) Write down all the words in the poem which rhyme with *spray*.
(b) Which of these words rhymes with *route*: rout, riot, boot, out, rot?

7. Use these joining-words in sentences: whether . . . . or, whenever, so that.

8. *Spelling* fish: her . . ng pla . ce sa . mon had . . ck
The convict stole a boat and e . caped from the i . land prison.
Give me a d . scrip . . . . of the str . . ger whom you saw car . . ing the box.

9. Change to (i) the Present tense (ii) the Past tense with *have* or *has*:
he became, it was, she came, I swam, they drank, you forgot.

10. Choose adverbs from this list to fit the sentences: politely, widely, happily, brightly, aloud, swiftly:
(i) The grass scatters its seed ——.
(ii) The children played —— in the park.
(iii) She laughed —— at the joke.
(iv) The messenger ran —— to the king.
(v) The lights were shining —— across the snow.
(vi) The man asked very —— about the lost football.

Now write a sentence of your own containing another adverb.

11. Write this in Direct Speech (the exact words spoken):
The small boy asked if he might borrow my pencil-sharpener.

12. Choose from each group the word which tells us what all the others are:
robins, thrushes, birds, corncrakes, cuckoos
willows, trees, poplars, elms, oaks, aspens
Town Hall, cinema, buildings, fire-station, theatre
carrots, cabbages, parsnips, vegetables, peas
cat, man, ceiling, desk, nouns, wood, planks
copse, clump, trees, forests, woods, plantations
river, stream, brook, water, lake, reservoir, pond
metals, iron, copper, steel, lead

13. Make four columns: *Family Father Mother Young*
Put these animals, birds, etc. in the "Family" column and fill in the other three columns: horses, geese, foxes, ducks, cattle, sheep.

14. What do we call a native of (a person born there):
Germany, Holland, France, Belgium, England, Denmark, China, Australia?

15. Use in interesting sentences: the white highway silver moonlight
nine tall aspens like gold the night wind.

Find Out

1. Find out what these words mean, then use one from each group in sentences:
scatter, shatter, scamper, scrape, chatter orchids, orchards, orchestra
dog-rose, dog-fox lovely, lively, lonely, lowly, loyal, loyalty, loyally
daisy, dairy, diary, dainty where, were, wear there, their, they're.

2. Find out the meaning of: as pale as death, a paleface, pale-faced; a tall order, a tall story; laugh up one's sleeve, no laughing-matter, a laughing-stock; He who laughs last, laughs longest.

3. Think of words which sound the same (or nearly the same) but which are spelt differently: mist, by, night, to, our, beech.
Give the meaning of your words.

4. SEASONS
Make a list for each season, putting in anything connected with that season, like the names of spring flowers, summer flowers and summer visitors (birds); migration, hibernation, the names of deciduous and coniferous trees, etc.

26 *A Secret Meeting*

Flavius stiffened, staring away to his left through the thin curtain of reeds that they had left between themselves and the outer world.

"What is it?" Justin whispered. And the other made a quick gesture for silence: then, timing the movement of his hand with a gust of wind, swayed back a few of the tall reeds. And Justin saw.

A man was standing not more than a spear-throw from them, his head turned to watch another who had that moment emerged from the willow-break farther inland. The water-cool light, growing every moment stronger, showed them the round buckler between his shoulders, and the wiry yellow gold of his hair and beard; and his sword-side being towards them, they could see the saex, the short Saxon thrusting-sword, in its wolf-skin sheath at his belt. And as the second man drew nearer, Flavius gave a long, soundless whistle. "Name of Thunder!" he whispered. "It is Allectus!"

Justin, crouching frozen beside him, was without any surprise. It was as though he had known.

Allectus had come up with the other man now. The Saxon said something in a low, angry growl, and he replied more loudly, "Aye, I know it is dangerous after cock-light. If I could have come sooner I would have done so—for my own skin's sake."

From *The Silver Branch* by Rosemary Sutcliff

The Silver Branch is about life in Britain under the Romans, when the Saxons had begun to raid our shores.

Comprehension

A 1. How many men are there in this extract from "The Silver Branch"?
2. Give their names, if you know what they are.
3. Which man asked a question?
4. What did his friend do, instead of answering?
5. (a) How many men did Justin see? (b) Where were they?
6. How do we know that Flavius and Justin were hiding in order to spy on someone?
7. What was a saex?
8. What was made of the skin of a wild animal?
9. How far away was the Saxon standing?
10. What is the meaning of: a thin curtain of reeds, a spear-throw, sheath; a long, soundless whistle; crouching; a low, angry growl?

B 1. What time of day was it?
2. (a) What are the two meanings of this phrase: "Justin, crouching frozen"? (b) Which meaning fits here?
3. Why should Flavius move back the reeds just as a gust of wind blew?
4. Describe the Saxon.
5. How do we know that Flavius knew the man who came out of the willow-break?
6. (a) Was Flavius surprised to see this man? (b) How do you know? (c) Was Justin surprised?
7. Allectus's secret meeting with one of his country's enemies means that he was (a Roman, a Saxon, loyal, honest, a traitor, trustworthy). Which?
8. (a) Who knew it was dangerous to come? (b) Why would he have come earlier, if possible?
9. Who was (a) angry (b) standing (c) crouching?
10. What is the meaning of: Flavius stiffened, a quick gesture, timing the movement, emerged, willow-break, water-cool light, round buckler, wiry, come up with the other man, after cock-light, for my own skin's sake?

Language

1. Find seven Compound words in the Comprehension passage "A Secret Meeting".
2. SUFFIX

   "Flavius gave a long, *soundless* whistle."

   We saw in Exercise 23 that we can add a PREFIX to the front of a word to make a new word: happy, *un*happy.

   We can make new words by adding letters to the END of some words:

   -less (without): sound, sound*less* (without sound)

   -ful (full of): grace, grace*ful* -ous (full of): mystery, myster*ious*

   -ling (little): duck, duck*ling*

   -er, -or, -ist, -ant, -ent (a person who does something): hunter, actor, violinist, servant, student.

   Sometimes we have to alter the spelling before we add the new ending:

   myster*y*, mysterious pian*o*, pianist serv*e*, servant stud*y*, student

   Remember: Letters added to the end of a word to make a new word are called a SUFFIX.

   Add to each of these words a suffix from the above list: act, farm, harp, sail, duck, care (2), goose (NOT gooseling), explore, assist, preside, attend.

   Use two of your new words in sentences.
3. What are these places: a city, hamlet, zoo, reservoir, granary, factory, hardware shop, an aviary?
4. Put these into their proper order, the smallest place first:

   continent, village, city, country, town, county, world.
5. Complete these similes: as pleased as ——, as green as ——, as black as ——, as safe as ——, as smooth as ——, as brown as ——, as clear as ——, as cool as ——, as good as ——, as right as ——.
6. *Find the Stranger:* whispered replied stiffened said answered
7. Use in short sentences: know, no, now, known, none.
8. Write a sentence containing a Proper noun (underlined) and the pronoun *who*.
9. Find out *all* the meanings of left, time, back, saw, stand.
10. Change this to Indirect or Reported Speech (*not* the exact words spoken):

    "The dawn is coming," Justin said to Flavius. "We must watch carefully now."
11. Make three lists headed *size*, *colour*, *shape* and put each of these words into the

correct list: square, crimson, fat, pink, oblong, mauve, enormous, circular, scarlet, height, cross, pied, oval, thick.

12. *Spelling* Spell these words, the meaning of which is given:
fort . . . . . ly: luckily   inter . . . .: speak when someone else is speaking
rec . . . ise: remember someone when you meet   fat . . . .: tiredness
f . . . ile: fruitful, not barren   pop . . . .: well-liked   a . . . s: pains
p . . ch . . .: buy   pig . . .: a bird   pun . . . . .: not late

13. Write S for *same* meaning, O for *opposites* in each pair:
(i) dawn, daybreak (ii) coming, arrival (iii) knife-edged, sharp (iv) slowly, rapidly (v) faint, loud (vi) emerged, disappeared (vii) tall, short (viii) whispered, shouted (ix) observe, watch (x) some, none.

14. Make the second pair agree in the same way that the first pair agree:

horses, strong	:	kittens, ——	lamb, young sheep	:	foal, —— ——
grass, green	:	daffodils, ——	tulip, flower	:	tiger, ——
wolves, wild	:	dogs, ——	sitting, chair	:	——, bed
iron, heavy	:	feathers, ——	breeze, gale	:	wren, ——

15. Use in interesting sentences: a spear-throw   the willow-break   thin curtain of reeds   a gust of wind   a low, angry growl.

Find Out

1. Find out what these words mean, then use one from each group in sentences: stiffen, stiff, stifle, stile, style, still (2), stilts   inland, island, inlet, Ireland, Iceland   sword, sward, swarm, swarthy   gesture, jester, guessed, guest, quest, question   buckler, buckle, buck (2).
2. Find out the meaning of: vanish into thin air, as thin as a rake; a short cut, to go short, short-tempered, at short notice, stop short, short-sighted, short-winded, the long and short of it, to fall short, shortbread, shortcake, short-handed, shorthand, in short, in shorts.
3. Think of words which sound the same (or nearly the same) but which are spelt differently: aloud, alter, berry, board, bolder, bough, break, ceiling.
Give the meaning of your words.
4. ROMAN BRITAIN
Find out about Julius Caesar's two visits (B.C.), the real invasion in 43 A.D., Watling Street (and others), Hadrian's Wall, the Picts and Scots, the Angles, Saxons and Jutes.

27

Fire!

At the end of the night, the chief hunter had issued his orders. The youngest boys had seized the fire with iron pikes and tallow torches and rushed off across the bush. At specific points they had started fires in the savanna, where there was dead wood or where a dry grass-track, running under the trees, would set the forest on fire. The bush thus kindled flared up, completely encircling the elephants and cutting off all escape.

At the height of noon the fire was raging everywhere in the wood; a curtain of high flames and smoke reached the sky. Trapped, Tarkwada's tribe, charging after their leader and smashing the trees in their way, looked for a way out by the stream but were horrified to see the remorseless fire still sweeping towards them.

They turned, terrified; desperately they strained up steep wooded hillsides. There was panic in their hearts and their blood raced madly as they gasped and fought for breath, winded with running. Fire was everywhere, in front, behind, blocking every way out of the forest. There was no question of being able to make a way through the tiny openings left for lesser game, antelopes, boars, and madly charging buffaloes, blinded by the smoke; they were only small gaps between giant trees and would have stopped an elephant. Hunters were posted there and struck down all that came within range of their arrows. The young Lobis especially enjoyed this sport.

From *Sama* by René Guillot

savanna: grassland.

Comprehension

A 1. When did the leader of the hunters say what had to be done?
2. (a) Who set fire to the grass? (b) How?
3. How did this set the forest on fire?
4. (a) What could not escape? (b) Why?
5. Tarkwada's tribe was a tribe of ——. What?
6. What curtain was there in the wood?
7. Why could Tarkwada's tribe not escape through the gaps between the trees?
8. Where were the hunters?
9. What did they do there?
10. What is the meaning of: chief hunter, dead wood, flared up, raging everywhere, horrified, terrified, blocking every way out?

B 1. Why was the fire "remorseless" (pitiless)?
2. What is the difference between running *across a bush* and across *the* bush?
3. Find near the beginning of the extract a word meaning "certain, special".
4. What (a) flared up (b) raged (c) rose high in the air?
5. Who were the young Lobis?
6. (a) What was like a game to them? (b) Would *you* call it a game?
7. What (a) was trapped (b) were blinded (c) raced madly?
8. Which of these are true?
   (a) Tarkwada was the chief hunter. (b) The fire was started by accident.
   (c) A herd of buffaloes was trapped. (d) The fire was started at dawn.
   (e) Many young Lobis were killed by elephants. (f) The young Lobis liked hunting.
9. Write down all the things which tell us that this did not happen in our country.
10. What is the meaning of: issued his orders, iron pikes and tallow torches, kindled, completely encircling, cutting off all escape, the height of noon, desperately, panic, winded with running, lesser game?

Language

1. Add a *different* suffix to *each* word to make new words:
   rest, remorse, courage, nest, art, conduct.

2. PARTS OF SPEECH

Fill in the missing words and give an example of each:

(i) **Nouns** are —— -words. Ordinary nouns are called —— nouns, like ——. Special nouns are called —— nouns, like ——.

(ii) **Adjectives** are —— -words, like ——.

(iii) **Verbs** are —— -words or a . . . . . s, like ——.

(iv) **Adverbs** tell us more about the ——, usually . . . it was done, like ——.

Remember: Nouns, adjectives, verbs and adverbs are called PARTS OF SPEECH.

When learning new words, always find out if there are other parts of speech connected with the words, like this:

noun: obedience (The obedience of the slaves . . . .)
adjective: obedient (The obedient slaves . . . .)
verb: obey (The slaves obey . . . .)
adverb: obediently (The slaves work obediently . . . .)

What are the adjectives, verbs and adverbs formed from brightness, fear, anger?

3. Who or what live in a convent, stable, hutch, fold, lodge?

4. *Spelling* Spell these IE or EI words:

(i) make a hole through: p . . . . .
(ii) a seaside p . . r
(iii) my nephew's sister: n . . . . .
(iv) above your head: c . . . ing
(v) to grasp or take hold: s . . . .
(vi) take or accept: r . . . . . .
(vii) great sadness: gr. . . .
(viii) a leader; most important: c . . . .

5. Which is the correct word:

(i) Our cat (come, came) home late.
(ii) (As, Has) the dog (bitten, bit, bite) you?
(iii) We have (chose, chosen, choose) our books.
(iv) I (drew, draw, drawn) a picture of a lioness.
(v) We (drunk, drank) our milk and went out (to, too, two) play.
(vi) We all (sung, sang) joyfully.

6. Change to Direct Speech:

The explorer said that he had found a new race of pigmies in the jungle.

7. What do these words mean: bought, brought; borrow, lend; lie, lay?

8. Fill in the gaps:

the young boys	the younger boys	the youngest boys
a dry grass-track	——	——
high flames	——	——

9. "antelopes, boars and madly charging buffaloes . . . Tarkwada's tribe . . ."
   (a) Which words are plural? What is their singular?
   (b) What do we call a group of (a) antelopes (b) buffaloes (c) elephants?

10. *Find the Stranger:* elephants herds antelopes buffaloes

11. Put in the correct prepositions:
    apologise —— the lady —— your bad behaviour; very proud — his success; different —— mine; agree —— someone —— do something; angry —— him; divide —— two, —— more than two; full—— water; meddle —— it.

12. Make the second pair agree in the same way that the first pair agree:

hunting, hunter	:	gardening, ——
train, journey	:	ship, ——
cart, horse	:	——, locomotive (engine)
plough, farmer	:	plane, ——
basement, attic	:	——, treetop
oak-trees, forest	:	apple-trees, ——

13. Write correctly:
    go now you young boys ordered the chief hunter set the grass on fire

14. What are *all* the meanings of turn, watch, light, show, round?

15. Use in interesting sentences: the youngest boys encircling fire was raging terrified a curtain of high flames.

Find Out

1. Find out what these words mean, then use one from each group in sentences:
   pikes (2), spikes, spokes, spoken tallow, fallow, furrow, furlong charging (2), chasing, charming, chanting, enlarging breath, breathe.

2. Find out the meaning of: too many irons in the fire, as hard as iron, in irons, an iron, ironmonger, strike while the iron's hot; a set-back, set about a task, weather set fair; set out, forth, or off; set sail, rain set in, set eyes on, dead-set against it, set on fire, set free.

3. Think of words which sound the same (or nearly the same) but which are spelt differently: wood, way, hearts, fought, boars, cereal, course, current.
   Give the meaning of your words.

4. FOREIGN ANIMALS
   Make a list of wild animals which live in other lands and can be seen in our country in zoos, like elephants, antelopes and buffaloes.

28 *The Harpist's Escape*

Towards midnight there was an interval between feasting and dancing, and the harpist was left alone, without bite or swallow, in a quiet corner overlooking the garden.

Suddenly he heard low thrilling words by his ear: "Vengeance will come. Vengeance will come."

He turned, and outside in the moonlit garden he could see a small brown bird which hovered and fluttered and seemed to invite him to follow. Stiff and tired as he was, he rose and left the palace, and still the bird withdrew before him, sometimes aloft in the air and sometimes trailing its wing along the path he should take. At the palace wall he stood hesitating, but, "Vengeance, vengeance!" cried the brown bird, motioning with its head and wings, and it now seemed no easier to return than go forward. On they went, over field and furrow, till the hillside soared before them . . .

At last they reached the top of the hill, where his exhaustion was so great that he sank to the ground to rest: and now for the first time the bird was silent. The moon slid behind a black cloud that climbed out of the east: instead of a wide vision he could hardly see his hand before him; and the splashing of a brook somewhere below warned him that it might be dangerous for him to make any move. It came into his head and heart how foolish he had been to follow the voice of a bird, and he remembered with dismay that he had left his harp behind him in the palace.

"I must return," he cried, "before the dancing starts!" But the thought of those cruel faces struck him with such horror that he could not move, and soon weariness and the dark overcame him and he slept heavily till break of day.

In the morning he arose and rubbed the sleep from his eyes. Then he rubbed them again and again, for when he looked towards the palace there was no palace there: only a huge, calm lake where walls and towers had been, and his harp floating towards him on the face of the waters.

From *Welsh Legends and Folk-Tales* by Gwyn Jones

Comprehension

A 1. A harpist is a harp-(player, mender, polisher, maker). Which?
2. When was there a time of rest for the harpist?
3. What refreshment was he given then?
4. What was said to him while he was resting?
5. (a) Was the moon shining at midnight? (b) How do you know?
6. Why did the bird trail its wing along the ground?
7. The feasting and dancing was in a ——. What is the missing word?
8. Why did the bird become silent?
9. When did the harpist awake?
10. What is the meaning of: midnight, the moonlit garden, hovered and fluttered, aloft, dangerous, foolish, must return, horror, weariness; a huge, calm lake?

B 1. What tells us that the feasters and dancers were not kind people: (i) in the first paragraph (ii) in the paragraph which is next to the last?
2. Vengeance means "revenge". What did the bird mean by "Vengeance will come."?
3. (a) Was there moonlight all through the night? (b) How do you know?
4. How can we tell that the harpist had been playing for a long time?
5. (a) Where did he nearly turn back? (b) Can you guess why?
6. (a) How do we know that the hill was very high?
(b) Why did the bird choose such a spot?
7. Why was it safer to keep still on the hilltop?
8. Why did the harpist decide not to go back?
9. (a) What happened to the palace? (b) What happened to the people in it? (c) Why? (d) Why do you think the harpist's harp came back to him?
10. What is the meaning of: an interval, low thrilling words, seemed to invite him to follow, the bird withdrew, over field and furrow, exhaustion, he remembered with dismay, overcame him, on the face of the waters?

Language

1. Put in the missing words:

Noun	*Adjective*	*Verb*	*Adverb*
pleasure	pleasant	——	——
——	agreeable	agree	——

2. VERBS 4

Present tense: I run or I am running

Future tense: I *shall* run, We *shall* run

He *will* run, You *will* run, They *will* run.

If we change from "shall" to "will" (I will, we will) we change the meaning:

I shall come early. I *will* come early!

The first sentence is a simple statement.

The second sentence shows determination: I am determined to come early.

Say what the difference in meaning is here:

(i) I shall climb that rock tomorrow. (ii) I *will* climb that rock tomorrow!

Fill in the missing words, *will* or *shall*:

(a) I —— be very grateful for your help.
(b) I —— not come with you! Nothing will make me come with you!
(c) We —— leave at 7 o'clock.
(d) We —— leave and no one can stop us!

3. Find out *all* the meanings of short, second, draw, long, skin, face, swallow.

4. *Find the Stranger:* hill harpist garden corner palace

5. Write the plural of: diary, dairy, donkey, monkey, key, buoy, toy, pony.

6. Find in your dictionary words beginning with *in* which mean:

(i) priceless (ii) cannot be seen (iii) not guilty (iv) breaking into someone's speech (v) a wound (vi) clever (vii) make bigger (viii) a query or question.

7. *Compound Words*

(a) Make new words by adding another *word* at the end of these words: plough, black, wind, tooth, ink.
(b) Do the same by putting another *word* at the front of these words: house, man, cup, tops, cloth.

8. *Apostrophe:* (a) What is an apostrophe? (b) What two things does it do?
(c) Give an example of each of its two uses.

(d) What do these mean: the harpist's work, the harpists' work, the bird's invitation, the birds' migration, this girl's school, this girls' school?

9. Put into alphabetical order: midnight, harpist, forward, garden, first, brown, stiff, bird, seemed, go, head, field.

10. Write this as one sentence by using pronouns:

The harpist followed the bird. The bird led the harpist to safety, away from the palace before the palace was destroyed with everyone in the palace.

11. *Spelling* What do we call these people (all the words ending in IST):

p . . . . . . (a piano-player) a . . . . . (a painter) d . . . . . . (looks after our teeth)
c . . . . . . (sells toothpaste, aspirin, etc.) t . . . . . . (goes on tours or trips)
f . . . . . . (sells flowers) v . . . . (a violin-player) m . . . . (drives a car)?

12. Use three in sentences: between *or* among, accept *or* except, teach *or* learn.

13. Write sentences, adding adverbs to these verbs: arose, looked, floating.

14. How do we spell the missing words? (advice, advise): Follow his good ——.
(practice, practise): There will be a netball —— tonight.
(prophecy, prophesy): The wise man said, "I —— disaster!"

15. Use in interesting sentences: towards midnight, in a quiet corner, in the moonlit garden, the top of the hill, floating towards him.

Find Out

1. Find out what these words mean, then use one from each group in sentences:
soared, roared, reared (2), reappeared
splash, slash, sash, slacken
return (2), retreat, reveal, revel, revenge
feast, beast, least, yeast
floating, fleeting, flattering, flattening, flapping, flipping, flopping.

2. Find the meaning of: face the music, a bare-faced lie, face to face, in the face of danger, pull a long face; break the back of a task, break camp, heartbreak, breaking-in a horse, breakfast (why?), break down (2), break out or free, break open, a breakwater (why?), breakers (why?).

3. Think of words which sound the same (or nearly the same) but which are spelt differently: break, soar, dear, die, fair, feet, fir, flew, flower.
Give the meaning of your words.

4. WALES
Find in your atlas: the Rhondda Valley, Cardiff, Swansea, Anglesey, Aberystwyth, Llanfair P.G. (Anglesey), Caernarvon, Snowdon.
What is the legend of Gelert, connected with the village of Beddgelert?

29 *Flannan Isle*

"Though three men dwell on Flannan Isle
To keep the lamp alight,
As we steered under the lee, we caught
No glimmer through the night!"
A passing ship at dawn had brought
The news; and quickly we set sail,
To find out what strange thing might ail
The keepers of the deep-sea light.

The winter day broke blue and bright,
With glancing sun and glancing spray,
While o'er the swell our boat made way,
As gallant as a gull in flight.

But, as we neared the lonely Isle;
And looked up at the naked height;
And saw the lighthouse towering white,
With blinded lantern, that all night
Had never shot a spark
Of comfort through the dark,
So ghostly in the cold sunlight
It seem'd, that we were struck the while
With wonder all too dread for words.

And, as into the tiny creek
We stole beneath the hanging crag,
We saw three queer, black, ugly birds—
Too big, by far, in my belief,
For cormorant or shag—
Like seamen sitting bolt-upright
Upon a half-tide reef:
But, as we near'd, they plunged from sight,
Without a sound, or spurt of white.

From *Flannan Isle* by W. W. Gibson

Comprehension

A 1. The three men who lived on Flannan Isle were (on holiday, sailors, lighthouse-keepers, town lamplighters). Which?

2. When had a ship brought news?
3. This happened in (spring, summer, autumn, winter). When?
4. What colour was the lighthouse?
5. (a) Was its warning light working or was it out? (b) What tells us in the first verse?
6. Why is there a seagull in this poem?
7. The three black birds were (blackbirds, cormorants, shags, unknown birds). Which?
8. What did they look like?
9. What happened to these three birds?
10. What is the meaning of: dwell, keep alight, steered, a passing ship, spray, a spark, ghostly, tiny creek?

B 1. Why did some men go to Flannan Isle?

2. (a) When did they set sail? (b) Why did they go at once?
3. What is a "blinded lantern"?
4. (a) What "spark of comfort" did the lighthouse usually give? (b) Why "spark of *comfort*?"
5. Who says the first four lines of the poem?
6. What does "the naked height" tell us about the island?
7. Why were the men who went to the island "struck . . . with wonder all too dread for words"?
8. Can you guess why the three mysterious birds come into the story of Flannan Isle?
9. Why did the sailors think these birds could not be ordinary seabirds?
10. What is the meaning of: we caught no glimmer, what strange thing might ail, o'er the swell, towering white, struck with wonder, the hanging crag, in my belief, sitting bolt-upright, a half-tide reef?

Language

1. Use *will* or *shall* in these sentences:
   (i) We —— be pleased to visit you on Saturday.
   (ii) I —— not listen to your ridiculous excuses!

2. AGREEMENT

Plural: Three *men dwell* or *live* on the island. *They keep* the lamp alight.
Singular: One *man dwells* or *lives* . . . . *He keeps* . . . .

Remember: Singular goes with singular, plural with plural:
One *man lives*: singular noun (man) with singular verb (lives)
Three *men live*: plural noun (men) with plural verb (live)

This sounds very easy but we must be careful with words like *each*, *everyone*, *everybody*, *no one*, *nobody:* all *singular*: Each of the men *was* hurt.

Remember: (i) When we think about people *one at a time*, the verb is singular: Neither David nor Stephen *has* answered. Each of the boys *was* punished.
(ii) When we think about people *together*, the verb is plural:
Both men *were* hurt. The farmer and his son *were* working hard.

Write these sentences correctly:
(i) Everyone (has, have) written letters.
(ii) Neither Susan nor Margaret (has, have) been late this term.
(iii) Each girl (was, were) given a prize.
(iv) There (was, were) many people waiting in the queue.
(v) Both boys (are, is) sorry.

3. What work do these people do: lighthouse-keepers, seamen or sailors, lawyers, blacksmiths, caretakers, carpenters, cashiers, chauffeurs, clerks, coastguards, detectives, drovers, steeplejacks, dockers, mechanics?

4. *Find the Stranger:* (Think of Parts of Speech) three queer black ugly birds

5. (a) Change to Indirect or Reported Speech:
   "As we steered under the lee, we caught no glimmer of light," he said.
   (b) Change to Direct Speech:
   I told my crew that I had decided to sail to Flannan Isle.

6. BOUGHT and BROUGHT

Remember: Brought is from the verb *bring*. *Bought* is from the verb *buy*.
Use *bought* and *brought* in sentences.

7. Use *bring* and *fetch* in sentences.
8. Put into alphabetical order: tree, though, three, the, through, tough.
9. Choose six people from Question 3 and say *where* they work.
10. What does the word *abbreviation* mean?
    What do these mean: Rev., Dr., Mr., Feb., Wed., it's, St. (2), a.m. (why?), p.m. (why?), P.S., R.A.F., A.D. (why?), J.P.?
11. (a) Which words in the poem rhyme with night, spray, crag? (Do not miss any.)
    (b) Which of these words rhymes with *niece*: nice, seize, fleece, please?
12. *Spelling* people: as . . stant, serg . . nt, attend . . ., superintend . . ., presid . . ., merch . . ., inspect . ., conjur . ., trait . ., auth . ., build . .
    Our dog is a very fr . . nd . . cre . . ure indeed.
    The stars are sh . . ing bri . . . ly tonight.
13. What are the adjectives formed from these nouns, like anger, *angry*:
    loneliness, strength, accident, adventure, anxiety, beauty, caution?
14. Draw an envelope and address it to your parents.
15. Use in interesting sentences: no glimmer a passing ship lonely island in the cold three queer, black, ugly birds.

Find Out

1. Find out what these words mean, then use one from each group in sentences:
    glimmer, glimpse, glitter, glisten, glint, glide, glider dawn (2), fawn (3)
    steer (2), gear (2), jeer, leer, mere (2), peer (2), pier, veer, weir, weird
    though, through, threw, thought, thorough wonder, wander.
2. Find out the meaning of: a bolt from the blue, to bolt (3); in cold blood, cold comfort, to have a cold, have cold feet (2), as cold as ice, cold-hearted, left out in the cold, cold-shoulder someone, throw cold water on a plan; look on the bright side, up bright and early, brighten.
3. Think of words which sound the same (or nearly the same) but which are spelt differently: isle, ail, o'er, creek, half-tide, sight, caught.
    Give the meaning of your words.
4. LIGHTHOUSES
    Find out all you can about lighthouses and lightships.
    What are these: Trinity House, the Lizard Light, Barrow Deep, Eddystone, the Nore, lenses, fog-signals?

30 An Accident

We went slowly along behind a heavy cart, which clanked and rattled under the dripping trees, with the hoofs of the horse moving with broad thuds in front. We passed over black patches where the ash flowers were beaten down, and under great massed clouds of green sycamore. At the sudden curve of the road, near the foot of the hill, I stopped to break off a spray of larch, where the soft cones were heavy as raspberries, and gay like flowers with petals. The shaken bough spattered a heavy shower on my face, of drops so cold that they seemed to sink into my blood and chill it.

"Hark!" said Lettie, as I was drying my face. There was the quick patter of a motor car coming downhill. The heavy cart was drawn across the road to rest, and the driver hurried to turn the horse back. It moved with painful slowness, and we stood in the road in suspense. Suddenly, before we knew it, the car was dropping down on us, coming at us in a curve, having rounded the horse and cart. Lettie stood faced with terror. Leslie saw her, and swung round the wheels on the sharp, curving hill-side; looking only to see that he should miss her. The car slid sideways; the mud crackled under the wheels, and the machine went crashing into Nethermere.

From *The White Peacock* by D. H. Lawrence

Comprehension

A 1. What was noisy?
2. What were (a) black (b) green?
3. What did Lettie and the man follow?
4. Where was the bend in the road?
5. What did the man do there?
6. What dropped down on his face?
7. What did Lettie suddenly say?
8. The car was coming (up, down, across, round, through) the hill. Which?
9. What stood in the car's way?
10. What is the meaning of: thuds, black patches, clanked and rattled, dripping trees, quick patter, slowness?

B 1. How can we tell that there had recently been a storm?
2. What do you think Nethermere was?
3. Why do you think Lettie and her companion stayed behind the cart?
4. (a) Who was the driver who hurried? (b) Why?
5. Why did Lettie and her companion stand in the road "in suspense" (anxiously)?
6. (a) Why did the car rush towards them? (b) Did it hit them? (c) What happened?
7. Who was (a) Leslie (b) Lettie?
8. What was (a) cold (b) sudden (c) shaken (d) heavy and slow (e) heavy and gay?
9. Explain this: "As I was drying my face . . ."
10. What is the meaning of: great massed clouds, ash flowers, painful slowness, having rounded the horse and cart, a heavy shower, Lettie stood faced with terror, looking only to see that he should miss her?

Language

1. Write correctly:

   (i) The children (writes, write) interesting stories.

   (ii) Each of the players (was, were) given a medal.

   (iii) Neither Janet nor Jane (was, were) ready.

   (iv) Both the carpenter and the plumber (was, were) working in our house.

2. JOINING-WORDS

   Joining-words join together parts of sentences or join two sentences into one:

   (i) We had jam, marmalade *and* honey on the table.

   (ii) We left the library *and* went home. (We left the library. We went home.)

   There are many *joining-words*: and, but, until, till, before, after, if, unless, neither . . . nor, although, because, etc.

   Remember: (1) *No* comma before *and*: see sentence (i) above.

   (2) We may leave out words when *and* or *but* join sentences: see (ii) above.

   (3) Joining-words are called CONJUNCTIONS (a junction is a joining-up).

   Use any of the conjunctions in the above list to complete these sentences:

   (i) He gave me the book —— I had worked well.

   (ii) The farmer decided to wait —— the shepherd came back.

   (iii) I cannot solve this crossword —— you help.

   (iv) Write your name on the list —— you wish to go on the trip.

   (v) —— the goalkeeper tried hard, he could not reach the ball.

3. "It moved with painful slowness . . ."

   The word *painful* means full of pain. What are the words which mean *full of* mercy, peace, hate, grace, beauty?

4. *Find the Stranger:* flowers cart raspberries larch sycamore

5. *Spelling* people: peas . . . oppon . . . account . . . edit . . doct . .

   At the beg . . . ing of the season I was not very good at swim . . . . in races.

   Take advant . . . of the C . . . . . mas holidays to do some Math . . . . . cs problems.

6. Complete these Past tenses, like I *ran*, I *have run*:

he began, he has ——	it bit, it has ——	it ——, it has blown
I broke, I have ——	we ——, we have drawn	it fell, it has ——
we ——, we had eaten	you ——, you had drunk	he ——, he had shaken

7. (a) Give the plural of: mist, flash, cry, arch,. reindeer.
   (b) Give the singular of: raspberries, hoofs, patches, heroines, mice.

8. What are the opposites of under, stopped, soft, heavy, gay, painful, slowness, downhill, cold, curving?

9. DO YOU REMEMBER?
   Find in the Comprehension passage, "An Accident": (a) an example of Direct Speech (b) 3 Proper Nouns (c) 3 Common nouns (d) 2 adjectives (e) 2 verbs (f) 2 pronouns (g) 2 adverbs (h) 2 prepositions (i) an exclamation.

10. "The shaken bough . . ."
    Note the spelling and pronunciation (sound) of *bough*.
    There are several different sounds which are all spelt OUGH. Think of another word ending in *ough* which rhymes with each of these words:
    bough, enough, thorough, cough, though
    Think of an *ough* word which rhymes with "shoe".

11. Change all masculine nouns to feminine nouns, making other changes that are necessary:
    (i) The man told his son to go home.
    (ii) The dog-fox carried off a cockerel.
    (iii) The bull, the stallion, the ram and the gander were going to the market.
    (iv) The Boys' Grammar School has a new headmaster.
    (v) The young prince asked his old grandfather to tell him the story about the duke who was a hero.

12. DICTIONARY WORK
    Find these words in your dictionary, then write down the meanings given there: boisterous, vacant, fertile, cautious, zinc, vagabond, epidemic, strenuous, courteous, efficient.

13. Put the words in Question 12 into alphabetical order.

14. Choose the correct words:
    different (to, than, from) the man (who, which, what) the dog (who, which, what) full (with, by, of) fell (off, of) went out (the, of the) room.

15. Make the second pair agree in the same way that the first pair agree:

wheel, spokes	:	ladder, ——
foot, man	:	——, horse
primrose, spring	:	rose, ——
schools, pupils	:	——, monks
train, platform	:	ship, ——
trees, forest	:	——, flock
gurgling, stream	:	——, bells
sailor, Navy	:	——, Army
November, December	:	January, ——
hill, hillock	:	river, ——

16. Use in interesting sentences: the dripping trees quick patter slid sideways near the foot of the hill clanked and rattled.

Find Out

1. Find out what these words mean, then use one from each group in sentences:
rattle, cattle, prattle larch, lurch, launch (2), lunch
bough, bought, brought, borough, boulder, bound (2), boundary
horse, hoarse cones, scones, scolds, scoffs exclamation, explanation
spray (2), pray, prey, pry (2), spry, sprightly, sprig, sprat, sprain.
2. Find out the meaning of: in someone's black books, things look black, black and blue, in black and white, black looks, blackberries, black-beetles, black currants, blackbirds, blackboards, the Black Death, a blacksmith.
3. Think of words which sound the same (or nearly the same) but which are spelt differently: frays, freeze, gamble, groan, meddle, missed, past, serial.
Give the meaning of your words.
4. TREES
Make a list of common British trees. Find out how to recognise them from their shape, their leaves and fruit.
What do these two words mean: deciduous and coniferous?